The Fragrant Pantry

FRANCES BISSELL is the author of numerous books and was *The Times'* food writer for thirteen years. Her articles have appeared in a wide range of publications in both the British and the international press, including *The New York Times, San Francisco Examiner, Boston Globe, Le Figaro, The South China Morning Post, Bangkok Post* and *El Diario de Jerez,* and magazines such as *Taste, A la Carte, Victoria* and *Food Arts.* She has written and presented two television series based in the West Country and appeared on a variety of TV shows in North America.

She has received the Glenfiddich Award for Cookery Writer of the Year in Britain, while her *Book of Food* won a James Beard Foundation Award in America. Frances Bissell has been guest chef in some of the world's leading hotels and restaurants, including the Café Royal Grill Room in London, the Mandarin Oriental in Hong Kong, the George V in Paris and The Mark in New York. She is a Fellow of the Royal Academy of Culinary Arts.

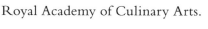

By the same author

A Cook's Calendar

The Pleasures of Cookery

Ten Dinner Parties for Two

Oriental Flavours

The Book of Food

The Real Meat Cook Book

The Times Cookbook

The Times Book of Vegetarian Cooking

Frances Bissell's West Country Kitchen

The Organic Meat Cookbook

An A–Z of Food and Wine in Plain English
    (with Tom Bissell)

Frances Bissell's Modern Classics

Entertaining

Preserving Nature's Bounty

The Scented Kitchen

The Floral Baker

The Fragrant Pantry

Frances Bissell

Serif
London

First published 2017 by Serif Books in association with OR Books/
Counterpoint Press. Distributed to the trade by Publishers Group West.

www.serifbooks.co.uk

10 9 8 7 6 5 4 3 2 1

British Library Cataloguing in Publication Data.
A catalogue record for this book is available from the British Library.

Library of Congress Cataloging-in-Publication Data.
A catalog record for this book is available from the Library of Congress

ISBN: 978 1 944869 50 2

Set in 11pt Bembo, Series style designed by sue@lambledesign.demon.co.uk

Typeset by Aarkmany Media, Chennai, India. Printed by McNaughton &
Gunn, Saline, Michigan.

Contents

For Tom

Preface

I was once invited to Colombia by the British Council to take part in a British Week, with gastronomy as the main theme. As well as curating a Food & Drink book exhibition, I gave a series of cookery demonstrations in Bogota, one of which was on *Cooking with Flowers,* Colombia being the home of an important flower-growing industry. I still have the faded photo-copied recipe sheets I prepared, including an English lavender pudding, a rose soufflé, rose junket, lavender sorbet, and lime flower and honey ice cream. But to give some historical context to my predilection for cooking with flowers, I opened my demo with an extract from the 1791 Warner edition of *Antiquitates Culinariae*, the earliest known collection of English recipes, with its origins in the Middle Ages. *"To preserve red rose leaves"* is as simple, straightforward and accurate now as when it was first written; *"Of the leaves of the fairest buds, take halfe a pound; sift them cleane from seeds; then take a quart of faire water, and put it in an earthen pipkin, and set it over the fire until it be scalding hot; and then take a good many of other red rose leaves, and put them into the scalding-water, until they begin to look white, and then strain them; and thus doe untill the water look verie red. Then take a pound of refined sugar and beat it fine, and put it into the liqueur, with half a pound of rose leaves, and let them seethe together till they bee enough; the which to know is by taking some of them up in a spoon, as you doe your cherries; and soe when they be thorow cold, put them up, and keepe them verie close".*

The smell of sugar and fruit cooking together in a large pan was a delicious part of my childhood, even though I complained about being scratched by brambles when we were sent off to pick wild blackberries in late summer before returning to school. And I can remember being rather dismissive of the glowing coral jelly my mother made from crab apples. Why could we not have shop-bought jam, like my school friends? But when I had a kitchen of my own, I soon experienced the satisfaction of making my own preserves, and the pleasure they give to friends and family. And I particularly enjoyed, and still enjoy, making jams and jellies from food gathered in the wild.

When staying in friends' houses for any length of time, I like to make myself feel at home by cooking, baking, and especially making preserves with whatever I find in their local market or forage in their garden. Often I would not have the proper equipment, especially for jelly making, and I can confirm that the up-turned stool with a scalded clean tea towel or pillowcase suspended from the legs makes a perfectly adequate jelly bag and rack.

This book is not about filling shelves and shelves with home-made preserves. Who amongst us has that kind of space in our kitchen? And who wants to spend hours peeling onions or strigging red currants? No, this is about using what you might find in your local farmers' market one Saturday morning, or what a friend might bring you from their house in the country. It's about thinking beyond a salad or a smoothie, and considering how you might preserve those fresh flavours for a while longer. It's about planning ahead to give your friends a small edible treat for a birthday or Christmas, something that is all your own work. It is easy, I promise you. There are no recipes calling for ten kilos of tomatoes, or a bushel of peaches — although if you are lucky enough to have such quantities, the recipes will adapt to accommodate them. With just a little fruit and some fresh edible flowers or floral extracts you can make two or three small jars of exquisite jelly. More unusual savoury preserves can be made with vegetables and certain flowers, and not all in jars. I have recipes for liqueurs and syrups, gin and grappa flavoured with flowers and fruit, and recipes for drying and freezing to preserve delicate flavours.

Preserving foodstuffs in times of plenty, to provide nourishment during lean times, has always been a part of the human experience. Making strawberry jam after a summer visit to a fruit farm is an atavistic memory of those times when our ancestors would preserve the seasonal gluts of fruit and vegetables for use in the winter. Of course we can buy strawberries from every part of the globe in winter, but who would buy expensive, and often tasteless, out-of-season strawberries to use in jam? No, the pleasure of making preserves is that we make them in season, when produce is at its peak and prices are at their lowest.

But the definition of 'seasonal,' 'home-grown,' and 'local' becomes wider and wider, with the strawberry and tomato season in England, for example, stretching from March to November, and 'new season' English asparagus on the shelves in September. A walk through North London streets in early November revealed thriving outdoor-grown olive trees with enough olives to make a harvest; a grape vine growing over the fence had ripe bunches of small black grapes; squashed fruit on the pavement had fallen from a laden fig tree a couple of weeks earlier; a jasmine bush was coming into flower for the second time; scented roses were in full bloom; lavender was still in flower and I saw nasturtium flowers tumbling over a rockery. I had picked my blackberries in July, fruit that always used to be associated with autumn. Wild garlic flower jelly was already made and put away in March. Tradition has it that sloes should be picked after the first frost. Had I waited that long, the birds would have eaten them long ago, as they were ripe for foraging in August. So these extended seasons with unusual growing patterns leads to some unexpected combinations; quince and rose petal jelly, for example. I give the recipe, however, (p.62) because somewhere, in one hemisphere or the other, at some time, someone might be able to make similarly unusual combinations. And if not, at least let them be inspirations for you to create your own flower and fruit preserves as you seize the day and make the most of an unexpected opportunity to produce a truly original creation.

Frances Bissell
London and Gozo
May 2016

Acknowledgments

I had always admired Serif Books, ever since Stephen Hayward introduced Edouard de Pomiane and Alice B. Toklas to a wider readership, and was delighted when he agreed to publish *The Scented Kitchen,* then *The Floral Baker* and finally, *The Fragrant Pantry.*

Stephen absolutely "got it" about cooking with flowers, using them as one uses herbs and spices, as another layer of flavouring. We would not only correspond about my books, but also about our foraging and cooking. When we met in the Groucho Club for editorial meetings, small bottles and jars would be exchanged – a pot of vintage rose petal jelly, a sample of an elderflower gin experiment.

I've worked with many excellent publishers but Stephen Hayward was quite simply the best. I owe him huge gratitude and feel privileged to be part of the Serif list, even though Stephen is no longer here to shepherd it to even greater things.

Justus Oehler and his colleagues at Pentagram and Sue Lamble have designed beautiful covers, text, and illustrations for my books, and they have my admiration and gratitude.

After Stephen's death, when this book's future was uncertain, five women stepped forward wit unstinting enthusiasm, encouragement, friendship, and support. I thank Julie Flint, Gay Hayward, Vicky Hayward, Jill Norman, and Michèle Roberts. I am immensely grateful to Jill for picking up where Stephen left off, and editing *The Fragrant Pantry* to completion. Any author would feel privileged to have had the benefit of her wisdom and insight, as I do. And I thank Vicky for finding me, and all Serif's authors, a new home with OR Books. I'm grateful to Colin Robinson, co-director at OR, for taking a personal interest in this book, and to his colleagues Valentina Rice, Alex Doherty and Jen Overstreet for their care in bringing *The Fragrant Pantry* to publication.

My love and thanks go, as always, to Tom for sharing my culinary adventures, my pots of jam, and my life for fifty years.

"The actual flower is the plant's highest fulfilment, and are not here exclusively for herbaria, county floras and plant geography: they are here first of all for delight".

John Ruskin

"One of the joys our technological civilisation has lost is the excitement with which seasonal flowers and fruits were welcomed; the first daffodil, strawberry or cherry are now things of the past, along with their precious moment of arrival. Even the tangerine – now a satsuma or clementine – appears de-pipped months before Christmas".

Modern Nature: The Journals of Derek Jarman

"Order extra salt for beans.

Shallots – use earthenware 7lb jars. Put lavender to dry. Refill bags. Linen room, bathroom cupboards, shelves".

Un-dated pencilled note found in a second-hand cookbook purchased by the author

Getting Started

This chapter will get you started and introduce you to the joys of making preserves, with suggestions for ingredients and equipment, all of which are readily available, inexpensive, and to be found in most kitchens. Cleaning copper is not my favourite pastime, so my kitchen is not adorned with an array of copper pots and pans, but I do treasure a well-made and sturdy copper preserving pan . . . to admire, and to use for pots of blue hyacinth and paper-white narcissi in winter. My jams and marmalades I make in a large, heavy, stainless steel pan with two handles.

At the beginning of each chapter I have included comments on techniques for making jams, jellies, chutneys, pickles, marmalade, salsas, and ketchups, as well as fruit-flavoured spirits and syrups. And there is more, besides. My floral-scented preserves include such delicacies as wild garlic flower pesto and jasmine tea-cured salmon, goats' cheese in olive oil and lavender, and a floral *Rumtopf*. These you will find in the final chapter.

My earlier book about the culinary uses of flowers, *The Scented Kitchen*, describes in more detail the properties of various flowers and their historical and cultural context. Here I restrict myself to the practicalities.

If you are using fresh flowers for your preserves, rather than floral essences, gather them on a dry day, late enough for the sun to have dried off the dew, but before it is hot enough to evaporate the fragrant essential oils.

Shake the flowers to remove any tiny insects and pollen. If the flowers need rinsing, do so quickly, in cold water, and lay the flowers to dry on two or three layers of paper towels.

Do not use edible flowers for culinary purposes if you think there is the slightest possibility that they may have been sprayed with pesticides or other chemicals.

Even if it smells as if it would taste good, do not cook with anything that you cannot positively identify as being edible.

If you suffer from hay fever or other allergies, it is probably best to avoid using flowers in the kitchen. This includes skin allergies, as handling certain flowers may exacerbate the condition.

Some flowers, such as lavender, have powerful properties, and should not be taken in large quantities, especially when pregnant.

Many of the flowers referred to in older cookbooks, such as violets, primroses, mallow, and cowslips, are wildflowers. Because the countryside is no longer carpeted with wild-flower meadows, those that remain are part of our dwindling natural heritage and need to be preserved. Certain species of wildflowers are protected by law and it is illegal to pick them. English Nature (www.english-nature.org.uk) and the Joint Nature Conservation Committee (www.jncc.org.uk) are among the best sources of information, highlighting the different Acts which protect certain flowers, and also the European Directives dealing with the same subject. Readers outside the United Kingdom will want to consult their own authorities about the gathering of wild flowers.

Some people feel that we should not pick any wildflowers whatsoever, others that a small picking, where there is an abundance, will not harm. Wildflowers should never be uprooted for transplanting in your own garden. It may be illegal to do so and it is certainly antisocial. Fortunately, specialist seed merchants can supply wildflower seeds, so there is no reason why you should not grow your own if you want to make violet syrup or cowslip wine.

The flowers of our herb gardens, which carry the more subtle scent of their "parent" plant, should not be forgotten. Rosemary, thyme, borage, marjoram, fennel, sage, bergamot, and many others can be used in jellies, liqueurs, and ketchups, and many of them are suitable for preserving by crystallising.

Which scented flowers?

Elderflowers

Ignore the dull leaves and rank twigs of elder trees and wait for the first creamy blossoms in spring. As you pick the delicate blooms, shake them lightly to remove any insect life and excess pollen and stow them loosely in a cotton bag as you continue your harvest. I prefer to use fabric because on occasion I have found that if I use a plastic bag, the flowers have become damp and discoloured by the time I reach home with them. The cotton absorbs any moisture.

If you have inadvertently picked any flower heads that are really infested with bugs, discard them immediately.

When I make syrup, jelly or cordial from the elderflowers, I always strain it through a fine cloth-lined sieve, which takes care of any tiny insects that might remain on the flowers, as well as the pollen, which makes the liquid cloudy.

The blossom itself has relatively little fragrance on its own. It is only when it is steeped in spirit or syrup or added to fruit for jam or jelly that the characteristic muscatel flavour is discernible.

Happy matches include gin, grappa, gooseberries, lemons, rhubarb, loquats, strawberries, and apples.

Fennel flowers

A scent redolent of the Mediterranean, although it also grows in temperate climates. I love the versatility of the fennel flavour. Most of my cooking with fennel flowers has been in the Maltese islands, where I pick bunches of them, together with borage and wild rocket, in the early summer, on a morning walk. I always manage to bring a small bag of the tiny yellow flowers back to London, so that I can preserve this sweet anise scent in my own kitchen for the winter months.

Happy matches include lemons, figs, pears, gooseberries, cucumber, and globe artichokes.

Hawthorn, myrtle, and apple blossom

These three delicate white flowers are very pretty, smell sweet and are attractive when strewn on a green salad. Their scent, however, is fleeting, and the best way to capture it is in spirit, such as the flower garden grappa referred to on p.114, or the Hedgerow Gin on p.109. Myrtle flowers are also used to flavour a liqueur, *crème de laurier*, which also includes bay leaves (*laurier* in French). Similar recipes appear on several web sites where *laurier* is translated as laurel; **laurel leaves are poisonous.** My recipe for Myrtle Ratafia is on p.105.

Lavender

L. officinale is the most fragrant of all lavenders, the most highly prized for the quality of its essential oils, which are used in the perfume industry as well as for culinary purposes.

Because of the strength of its volatile oils, lavender should be used sparingly. It should be noted that lavender has powerful therapeutic properties and should only be used in medicinal quantities under medical supervision.

For me, the scent of lavender is equally at home with the sweetness of a lemon curd and the savouriness of a tomato salsa or a salty tapenade.

Happy matches include tomatoes, shallots, blackcurrants, blueberries, raspberries, blackberries, lemons, and oranges.

Jasmine

The white, star-shaped, highly scented *Jasminum officinale*, which is also the flower used to scent jasmine tea, is edible. So too is the larger flower, also a member of the Oleaceae family, often found in more Mediterranean climates, the *Jasminum grandiflorum*. In traditional medicine, jasmine has been used in many cultures both as a calmative and as an aphrodisiac, as well as for curing coughs.

As it is so highly scented, jasmine is rewarding to work with, but the flowers are delicate, and must be picked early in the morning before the essential oils evaporate.

Happy matches include rum, vodka, mangoes, guavas, limes, bananas and apple.

Linden or lime flower

Linden flower, or *tilleul*, is much used in France for tisanes and infusions, as well as stronger drinks. *Ratafia de tilleul* used to be made in the Drôme, where the most fragrant French blossoms come from. At the right time of year, I am often stopped in my tracks on a morning walk in north London by a wave of intense fragrance as the breeze ripples through some lime trees, sadly too tall for me to reach the blossoms.

Do try these fragrant flowers in the kitchen; they are easy and rewarding to use, and widely available, fresh in June, just after the elderflowers, or dried at other times of the year. It is certainly worth harvesting the blossom and drying it for use throughout the year.

Tilia cordata and *T. platyphyllos* produce the most fragrant flowers, ideal for flavouring syrups which can then be used for sorbets, ice creams and other delights and also for combining with fruit in delicate jams and jellies.

Happy matches include loquats, gooseberries, gin, peaches, apricots and nectarines.

Marigold

The pot marigold, *Calendula officinalis*, a native European plant, is the flower I use, not the French or African marigold.

Marigold's culinary uses have long been known, especially as a colouring. The petals contain carotene and lycopene, and have often been used as an inexpensive substitute for saffron. They have also been used to colour cheese and butter. The petals give a subtle, spicy flavour and golden colour to whatever they are used with.

Happy matches include nasturtiums, olive oil, garlic, and cheese – as in Pesto on p.162 – and, for their obvious colour match, apricots, and peaches.

Orange blossom

The scent of orange blossom always used to remind me of Jerez, where the streets are lined with orange trees, but since I began spending part of each year on the island of Gozo, the scent reminds me of a small orange grove on the slopes of the Marsalforn Valley above Ta' Frenc restaurant, where the trees are protected by tall stands of bamboo from the salty wind which blows in from the north. I know someone on the island who makes her own orange flower water on Gozo – a slender link to Malta's historic orange cultivation and orange flower water industry. My favourites, apart from the Gozitan product, are those from the Lebanon.

Happy matches are numerous and include, of course, oranges and other citrus fruit, but also carrots, dates, figs, bananas, and chocolate.

Pinks and clove carnations

These have always been one of my favourite flowers and were among the first flowers I used in public, as it were, when I was guest chef at London's Intercontinental Hotel at Hyde Park Corner for two weeks one summer. The carnation ice cream was something of a shock to the pastry kitchen, but a delight for the customers.

The gilly flower, or July flower – older names for carnation – denotes that family of sweetly scented flowers including clove pinks, phlox, Sweet Williams, and the stiffly formal carnation. In all, to a greater or lesser degree, the spicy smell of cloves is their distinguishing feature, but enveloped in a cloud of sweet fragrance.

Happy matches include apples, almonds, pears, strawberries, and cherries.

Roses

The best roses to use are those in the deep pink to dark red spectrum, and they must be of the old-fashioned scented varieties, such as *Rosa officinalis*, the apothecary's rose, *R. gallica*, *R. damascena* and *R. centifolia*. Wild roses such as *R. rugosa* have a wonderful deep colour and rich fragrance, but, having so few petals, a large number of roses are required.

Note that rose petals will not soften if you cook them in syrup. The best way to deal with them in jelly making is to cook them with the fruit before straining the extract or let the hot fruit liquid drip through the muslin onto the rose petals, which will wilt, if not cook them, then bring liquid and petals to the boil before adding the sugar.

Happy matches include all the summer berry fruits, especially strawberries and raspberries, but also cherries, green and purple figs, blueberries, rhubarb, apples, and quince, lychees, champagne, and rosé wine.

Saffron

Saffron comes from the saffron crocus, *Crocus sativus*, not to be confused with *Colchicum autumnale*, the autumn crocus, which is sometimes misleadingly referred to as meadow saffron, although it is rarely to be found in the wild any longer, more usually as a garden plant. Confusingly, both have bright pale purple flowers and bloom in the autumn, but **the autumn crocus is poisonous.**

Most of the saffron we buy is from La Mancha in Spain, but some comes from Egypt, Greece, Iran, Kashmir, India and Morocco. There is a modest revival of saffron-growing in Britain, principally in Devon, Wales, Norfolk and Essex, which was saffron's original English home in the Middle Ages.

Saffron is not an easy ingredient to weigh or measure, and so I suggest "a pinch of saffron filaments" in most of the recipes, which is the amount taken up by finger and thumb; if you were to count out the filaments, they would number about 20. I am assuming that readers will be using dried saffron, not the freshly plucked stigma of *Crocus sativus*.

The dried petals of the safflower, a member of the thistle family, from which safflower oil is derived, has something of the colour and appearance of dried saffron, although not the flavour, and is sometimes passed off for the costlier spice in many markets and bazaars.

Happy matches include rum, vodka, gin, quince, pears, apples, shallots, and artichokes.

Violets, cowslips, and primroses

To have enough of these delicate wildflowers for using in preserves, realistically you will need to plant the flower seeds and grow your own, even if you "know a bank where the nodding violet★ grows." **Despite their name, colour and appearance, African violets or St. Paulia are not of the viola family and are not known to be edible.**

Violet flowers are so delicate in fragrance, and so difficult to obtain in any quantity, that I hesitate to combine them with other ingredients. Primroses I preserve by crystallizing for use on cakes and tarts, and I restrict myself to a pot or two of violet jelly. Traditional English recipes for cowslip wine required "8 lbs of cowslip heads," a sight impossible to imagine today.

Dried flowers, floral essences, and commercial floral liqueurs and syrups

Whilst I prefer to preserve fresh fruit and vegetables with their matching seasonal flowers, I try not to be a purist about it, otherwise some glorious flavours would be missed. Seville oranges and lavender are a perfect blend for marmalade, but one is in season in January and the other in June. The answer is to use dried flowers, floral essences and other edible commercial floral preparations.

Lavender farms, especially, are an excellent source of culinary floral material, including fresh flowers. Garden shops, gift shops attached to country houses and other horticultural establishments are all useful sources of floral ingredients. A search of the internet will find those most convenient for you.

In addition, some of the larger supermarkets as well as specialist food shops sell the essences. And for commercial liqueurs and syrups, the internet is the best source for finding the products in your area. Try www.diffordsguide.com for information about commercial and artisan producers. **Marie Brizard** is the best-known commercial brand for violet liqueur, but **Briottet** and **Combier** are also ones to look out for. They are available online, as well as in stores which carry a strong range of French wines and liqueurs. Other artisan brands can often be found, as well as non-alcoholic flower syrups. Liqueur or syrup can be used in the recipes on p.50 and p.68. And, of course, the famous Lakeland Ltd is an excellent source for essences, as well as a wide range of equipment for preserving.

You may also find dried rose petals, camomile, and linden flowers in establishments which sell tisanes and loose teas.

Some flowers can be dried at home. Fennel flowers can be gathered when any dew has evaporated, spread on a clean tea towel and left in a warm, dry place until perfectly dry. Crumble the flowers into a jam jar, cover with the lid and store in a cupboard. Lavender flowers can be dried in the same way. Both retain their scent and flavour very well for up to a year.

I find rose petals, carnations, and other soft petals more difficult to dry in this way, as they often oxidize before they are dry. Instead, I spread them on a baking tray lined with baking parchment and dry them in the oven on the lowest setting with the door propped open, for as long as it takes, which will depend on how many flowers, how thick the petals are, and how dry they were when you put them in the oven.

An important note on almonds, apricots, peaches, etc.

Do not include the kernels when making preserves with apricots, peaches, or plums, nor use bitter almonds. Instead use pure almond essence. The cyanogenic glycosides present in bitter almonds and in the kernels of stone fruit such as apricots, peaches, plums, and nectarines, as well as apple and pear pips, are unlikely to be destroyed by cooking. The kernels contain significant amounts of these compounds and, as they are natural products, the amount they contain will vary. Despite what many cookery books state, these toxins are not destroyed in cooking, and as a general practice we should not be adding cyanide to our food.

Ordinary "sweet" almonds are safe to use; except, of course, for those persons who have nut allergies.

Preserving techniques and equipment

Sugar, salt, vinegar, and alcohol are all natural preservatives. We can use them alone, or in combination, and they all work in the same way, by providing a hostile environment for the bacteria, yeasts, and mould that would otherwise cause spoilage and fermentation of fruit, flowers, and vegetables in jams, jellies, pickles, chutneys, and other preserves.

Water is the perfect medium to encourage bacteria to grow, and as fruit and vegetables are largely made up of water, the object in preserving them is to replace the water with a high concentration of sugar, vinegar, salt, or alcohol in various combinations, or, in the case of drying, to remove the water altogether. Long, slow cooking also aids this process because water evaporates during cooking.

So **chutneys**, which are generally cooked for a long time, release much of their water content and need less vinegar than pickles. The reason for this is that for the most part, **pickles** are raw or only lightly cooked, and therefore need a heavy dose of vinegar to preserve them, as well as an initial brine bath to draw out the water.

Jams and **jellies** have about an equal proportion of fruit and sugar, and this high sugar concentration ensures that mould will not occur.

Do not be tempted to reduce the sugar content of any of these preserves, with the aim of reducing the calories contained in them. A reduction in sugar may lead to fermentation, spoilage, and mould.

Ingredients required in making preserves

Alcohol

For preserving fruit, such as the *Rumtopf* recipe on p.154, and making flavoured liqueurs and spirits, such as the fig and fennel flower vodka on p.111, a neutral inexpensive vodka is best; you do not need to invest in a premium brand.

For some of the floral liqueurs and spirits, I find gin provides the best base, and for these I generally choose a supermarket's own label gin, which offers a neutral background for me to "dress up" with floral flavours.

And if rum is required, I recommend a white rum. It is also worth experimenting with grappa and for this, again, I recommend an inexpensive neutral one, or a simple grappa di moscato.

Pectin

This is a form of carbohydrate contained in the cell walls of fruit and is the substance which makes jams and jellies set or 'gel' when combined with sugar. As the fruit ripens, the pectin diminishes, so it is important to choose fruit that is just ripe or slightly under-ripe. Over-ripe fruit is often sold at bargain prices, which is fine for syrups and ketchups, but, as it will not set well, it is not worth buying for jams and jellies.

Some fruits contain plenty of pectin; others have far less and require the addition of extra pectin, in the form of pectin-rich fruit, or liquid or powdered pectin. Liquid or powdered pectin is made from apple or citrus trimmings, such as peel, seeds and pith; the best is made from apple.

Alternatively, sugar which already contains pectin and citric acid can be used. It is sold as 'jam sugar'.

When making floral jellies without any fruit "background." you need to add pectin, as flowers contain no pectin.

Acidity is also required to assist in releasing the natural pectin from fruit. Most fruits with high pectin also have high acidity, except for pomegranates, which are low in pectin but have medium to high acidity. Citrus fruits are high in acidity, as are black, red and white currants, and, surprisingly, plums. Lemon juice is used to provide any extra acidity needed for fruit such as strawberries and tropical fruit.

A guide to the pectin content of fruit

High

Apples, blackcurrants, clementines, crab apples, cranberries, damsons, gooseberries, grapefruit, guavas, kumquats, lemons, limes, oranges, plums, quinces, red currants, white currants

Medium

Apricots, blackberries, blueberries, grapes, greengages, logan-berries, prickly pears, raspberries, tomatoes

Low

Cherries, figs, kiwi fruit, lychees, mangoes, melons, passion fruit, peaches, pears, pineapple, pomegranates, rhubarb, strawberries

Home-made pectin extract

When making apple pies or sorbets, do not throw away the peel and cores. Instead, put them in a nonreactive saucepan, cover with water and simmer for 50 to 60 minutes, keeping the water topped up. Crush the peels with a potato masher then let the liquid drip through a muslin-lined sieve. When cool, store the liquid in a suitable container in the freezer until needed.

When cranberries are in season, I prepare some in the same way and make a red pectin-rich extract which is ideal for using with low-pectin red fruit such as strawberries and cherries.

Sugar

The best sugar for making jams and jellies is that with the largest crystals, as this dissolves slowly, minimizing scum and producing a nice clarity in the finished product. Therefore choose granulated sugar, which is an excellent all-round sugar, whatever preserves you are making. Preserving sugar, which has extra-large crystals, is even better. For chutneys, which are generally thick, opaque and quite dark, you can use an unrefined sugar, such as Demerara or moist brown sugar/light muscovado sugar. Jam sugar, which contains pectin and citric acid, is a boon when making jam from low-pectin fruit such as strawberries and figs because the preserve always sets when you follow the directions on the sugar bag.

Flower sugar

Most of my floral preserves use fresh flowers, but occasionally, when the fruit and flower season do not coincide, for example, it makes sense to use flower sugar. In an airtight container, this can be stored in a dark place and it will retain its flavour for about a year, until the flower season comes round again.

You will want to experiment with proportions according to which flowers you are using. Lavender will scent a larger amount of sugar than jasmine, and jasmine will scent a larger quantity of sugar than roses, for example. Roses, lavender, rosemary flowers, and clove pinks or carnations are the flowers I use when making floral sugars. Other flowers, such as elderflowers and jasmine, I prefer to preserve as syrups.

Even if you have only a small quantity of flowers, a couple of roses, or half a dozen sprigs of lavender, it is worth making some flavoured sugar.

Rose petal sugar

Rather than give quantities which may be unrealistic, an indication of proportion is probably more useful. One part rose petals will scent and flavour 4 to 5 parts sugar.

Heavily scented rose petals, red or deep pink – see p.19
Granulated sugar

Spread the rose petals in a single layer on a clean tea towel or kitchen paper and leave to dry for 12 hours. Put them in a food processor with the sugar and process until the mixture is well blended. Unless you want the sugar for immediate use, it is important that the flowers are dry before you grind them, otherwise your food processor will be a mass of sugar paste before you know what has happened.

Lavender sugar

As in the previous recipe, an indication of proportion is probably more useful than prescriptive measurements. Bearing in mind that lavender is more strongly scented, I use one part lavender for 6 to 8 parts sugar.

Fresh lavender flowers
Granulated sugar

When making lavender sugar, follow the method above. For the purest colour, you need to choose lavender in full bloom and pick off each individual flower. If you simply separate from the stalk the flowers enclosed in the sepals, you will get a greenish sugar. The same happens with syrup.

Salt

My favourite salt is coarse sea salt, and I use this for all my preserves, both for the brine bath for pickles, and the flavouring of salsas and chutneys. Kosher salt, preserving salt and coarse rock salt can also be used. The reason for choosing a coarse salt, especially when brining, is that these do not contain the anti-caking additives found in many brands of fine salt, which can lead to distorted flavours and cloudiness in the brine.

Acid

Commonly used acids are vinegar and lemon juice. Lemon juice is more acidic than many vinegars, but has less effect on flavour, and you can use bottled lemon juice.

The vinegar used should be at least 5% acid. Pickles are best made with distilled malt vinegar, as it is strong and clear. Chutneys can use one of the darker vinegars, such as cider vinegar or red wine vinegar. However, there is now a huge range of vinegars from which to choose, and it is worth experimenting. Sherry vinegar is dark and strong, and will add distinction to your chutneys. Moscatel vinegar, made from sweet wine, is a delicate product, and useful when making spiced fruit preserves and more delicate chutneys.

Acid is corrosive when in direct contact with metal, so when you pot pickles and chutneys you should ensure that you are using vinegar-proof lids. This is one case where it is probably worth investing in new preserving jars, especially as some preserves need to be processed by the water-bath method (p.33) if you are planning for longer storage.

Here are a couple of useful vinegar recipes for pickling. You can adapt the spicing if you want to create new recipes.

Sweet vinegar

Bring the vinegar and spices to the boil in a nonreactive saucepan, stir in the sugar, and, when dissolved, boil for 1 minute. Remove from the heat, cover and leave to infuse for 3 to 4 hours. Then use as directed, or strain and bottle for future use.

makes 1 litre/1 quart

1 litre/1 quart white wine vinegar
1 cinnamon stick
4 cloves
4 crushed cardamom pods
500 g/1 lb/2 cups granulated sugar

Spiced vinegar

Put the vinegar, spices, and salt in a nonreactive saucepan, bring to the boil, stir in the sugar and, when dissolved, boil for 1 minute. Remove from the heat, cover, and leave to infuse for 3 to 4 hours. Then use as directed or bottle for future use.

makes 1 litre/1 quart

1 litre/1 quart distilled malt vinegar
1 teaspoon black peppercorns
1 teaspoon allspice
1 teaspoon coriander seeds
1 teaspoon cumin seeds
1 teaspoon blade mace
1 cinnamon stick
4 cloves
4 crushed cardamom pods
1 teaspoon salt
125 g/4 oz/½ cup granulated sugar

Equipment required for making preserves

Jam jars and others

Jams and jellies, because of their stable nature and good keeping qualities, can be potted in "second-hand" jars, that is, jars which may previously have contained jam, honey or mustard, for example. You can re-use the lids, provided they are not buckled, pierced, or otherwise damaged, and provided that you sterilise them first.

Any preserves which require processing in a boiling water bath should, ideally, be potted in new jars. Certainly they should have new lids and closures. The USDA has advised that Kilner jars and Le Parfait jars, with the glass lid, clamp, and rubber sealing ring, are no longer considered suitable, despite their still being available and in use, both commercially and domestically. The recommended jars have flat lids which fit flush to the rim of the jar, a non-metallic lining and an integrated rubber seal. They also have a separate screw band which is screwed, but not tightly, into place before processing. It is easy to tell that a vacuum has been formed, and the processing successful, because the lid will depress in the middle. When the jar is opened and the lid prized off, the vacuum is broken and the lid makes a slight popping sound.

All jars, lids, corks, and closures should be sterilised before use.

For domestic use, it is still possible, in many places, to buy the simplest seals for jam and jelly jars, which are wax discs and cellophane covers secured with a rubber band. When choosing the right size for the jar, simply place a disc, wax side down, on the surface of the jam or jelly. Moisten a cellophane disc and place it, wet side up, over the jar. Secure it round the neck with a rubber band. As the cellophane dries, it shrinks and creates a tight seal. It is important that you wipe the neck of the jam jar clean of any spills, otherwise there will not be a good seal.

Generally I find that jams and jellies sealed with cellophane covers dry out and firm up sooner than preserves sealed with lids.

For the recipes in the book, especially the jams, jellies, and marmalade, I have usually used 400 g/14 oz re-used jars, as these are what most of us save when we have finished the contents. That said, even a glance at my own second-hand jars show that they come in many sizes, and my batches of preserves will often come in a variety of jars; ex-honey jars and peanut butter jars, which tend to be 340 g/12 oz, erstwhile mayonnaise jars of 400 g/14 oz and 225 g/8 oz jars that once held skinned red peppers. However, from the yield indicated in the recipe, you will be able to calculate how many of your own jars the preserve with fill. For example, the four 400 g/14 oz jars of Rhubarb, pear, and clove pink jam on p.42 can be exchanged for eight 200 g/7 oz jars, or three 500 g/1 lb jars with a little bit left over for the jam dish to be used right away.

If you are making preserves for presents, fairs or fund-raisers, it is strongly advised that you use the USDA-recommended jars.

To sterilise jam jars

If you are preparing a large batch of preserves, the easiest way is to put all the jars and lids in the dishwasher and put it on the hottest cycle. When the cycle is over, transfer the hot jars with tongs to a work-top covered with a clean tea towel.

Alternatively, simmer the jars and lids in boiling water for 15 minutes. You can also use the oven. Heat it to 220°F/110°C, put the jars and lids in and leave them for 15 minutes. Switch the oven off and leave the jars inside until you are ready to fill them with hot preserves. If filling them with cold preserves, e.g., pickles, remove them from the oven straight after they have been sterilised to allow them to cool. Again, use tongs to remove them and place on a covered work-top ready to receive the preserves.

Jam funnel

This wide-mouthed funnel is a very useful gadget that sits
inside the neck of the jam jar you are filling, thus avoiding
sticky spills down the side of the jar and on its neck, as well
as splashed hands. If you bottle syrups, ketchups, and cordials,
it is also useful to have a small funnel which will fit inside a
bottle neck.

Jelly bag and rack

This is a muslin bag designed to be suspended from a four-
cornered plastic rack which you secure on the rim of a
large wide bowl or jug. The muslin bag is first scalded with
boiling water before being suspended, and then you ladle
in the cooked fruit pulp when making jelly. The muslin is
fine enough to allow just the clear liquid to drip through,
ensuring a bright jelly.

It is possible to improvise and tie a thin scalded tea towel from
the four legs of an upturned stool, with the bowl in the middle.
I have done this countless times, and it works perfectly well.

Large saucepan with lid and trivet

This is essential equipment for the boiling water bath in which
preserves are processed in order to give them longer shelf life.
You can also use a fish-kettle as this has a false bottom, which
keeps the jars from the base of the pan and in contact with
direct heat.

Small (200 g/7 oz) or squat (500 g/1 lb) jars will fit a fish
poacher. This is a useful container for a water bath, since it will
fit across two burners on the stove, and will hold several jars.

Long-handled wooden spoon

This simply allows you to stir the mixture with less risk of the
hot mixture splashing your hand.

Muslin

When flavouring preserves with flower petals that you wish to extract before potting, it is a good idea to tie them in a small square of scalded muslin, which can easily be removed. You can buy a length of muslin and cut it into small squares to keep on hand for this purpose. You can also use tissue tea bags, which are sold in some specialist shops for filling with loose tea.

Nonreactive bowl

It is best to use a glass or plastic bowl for a brine bath or soaking ingredients in vinegar overnight when making pickles, as these do not corrode when in contact with salt and acid.

Nonreactive pan

Because of the amount of acid in fruits, and with the addition of vinegar for chutneys and pickles, it is essential to use a pan that will not corrode. The best are heavy-gauge stainless steel, which most of us use anyway. This is easy to clean and it is a good conductor of heat. Aluminium pans should not be used, as the metal reacts with acid and causes a chemical change to take place. The best pans for cooking preserves are large and wide. The mixture should not come more than halfway up the side of the pan, otherwise it is likely to boil over. A wide surface area ensures faster evaporation, so setting point is reached more quickly. A copper preserving pan, though very attractive, is not essential. You can also use specially tempered heatproof glass pans, such as Pyrex and Corningware, but these are not such good conductors of heat.

Plastic sieve

You will need this if you are making ketchup. Once the ingredients have been cooked to a pulp, they need to be sieved before bottling. Because the ketchup contains acid, a metal sieve should not be used.

Sugar thermometer

A thermometer is the surest way of testing when jam and jelly has reached its setting point. The temperature will be 221°F/105°C.

Tongs

Use these for handling jars which have been sterilised, and for removing jars from the boiling water bath once processed.

Water-bath processing

If you want to keep your preserves for a year or two, then they should be processed in a boiling water bath, which sterilises the contents of the jar, and seals them in a vacuum.

Low–acid foods require special processing techniques and equipment for canning or bottling which fall outside the scope of this book.

Sterilise your glass preserving jars and lids (see the note on p.29 about jars) after first checking that there are no chips or cracks on the neck of the jar, as this would prevent a seal from forming. Fill the hot, clean jars with the hot preserve. Wipe the jar rims with a clean, damp paper towel; anything sticky adhering to the rim would prevent the jars from sealing. Put on the lids and lightly screw on the metal bands.

Place the jars on a rack or trivet in your chosen water bath (see note on Large saucepan on p.31) of simmering water, ensuring that the jars do not touch each other or the side of the pan. Add boiling water to cover 2-5 cm/1-2 inches above the jar tops and bring the water to a rolling boil. Set the timer for the recommended processing time. Add more boiling water if necessary during the processing to keep the jars covered.

The processing time will be 15 minutes for 500 g/1 lb jars or bottles of salsa or ketchup, or 25 minutes for 500 g/1 lb jars of solid ingredients such as peaches. 1 litre/1 quart jars will need 25 and 30 minutes respectively.

At end of processing time, switch off the heat and use tongs to remove the jars from the water bath. Place the jars right-side up on a rack or work-top covered with a clean towel and allow them to cool. Do not tighten the screw bands. As the contents of the jar cool, they shrink and a vacuum is formed, creating sterile anaerobic or oxygen-free conditions in which bacteria does not survive. You can tell the jar is sealed if the lid is depressed in the centre and does not move.

Remove the screw bands from the sealed jars and wipe the jars with warm, soapy water, then rinse and dry them without disturbing the lid. Label and date the jars and store in a cool, dark, dry place.

If a vacuum has not formed, refrigerate the contents of the jar and use as a fresh product, eating within a week.

A Note on Measurements and Volumes

I have used metric, imperial, and American measurements and volumes. In more and more countries, sugar, spirits and vinegar – all important ingredients in this book – are sold in 500 gram and 1 kilo bags, in 350 ml, 500 ml, 750 ml and 1 litre bottles. British readers may find it helpful to remember the little ditty my friend Julia Child would often quote to me:

> A pint's a pound the world around, just as it oughta'

> Except in Britain where a pint is a pound and a quarter.

I have opted for the practical approach and given a set of measurements which makes sense, rather than provides exact equivalence. It is important to follow one set of measurements within the recipe, and not switch between American, metric, and imperial.

What went wrong?

Occasionally the preserve does not turn out as you had hoped. There are a number of reasons but if any of your preserves show signs of spoilage, through mould or fermentation, if they smell bad when you open them, or if the jar lid is "blown" or swollen, then discard the preserve immediately, carefully wrapping it and safely disposing of it.

Jellies and jams

The jelly is cloudy

There are several possible causes. The juice was not properly strained and contained particles of pulp. If the fruit was too under–ripe, it may have set too quickly. The jelly was allowed to stand before being poured into the jars or it was poured in too slowly.

There are crystals in the jelly

You may have used too much sugar in the mixture, or cooked it too slowly, too long, or, sometimes, too little. Crystals may also form on top of a jar of jelly that has been opened and allowed to stand; these crystals are formed by evaporation. Grape jelly may develop tartrate crystals, as do some white wines occasionally: they are not harmful.

The jelly or jam is too soft

There may be too much juice in the mixture or too little sugar. The acid level in the mixture may not be high enough or you might have cooked too big a batch of fruit at one time.

There is mould on the jelly or jam

Air and, with it, bacteria, has entered the container through an imperfect seal. Do not simply discard the mould and consume the rest of the jar's contents, but **discard the entire jar.** Remember to always use recommended canning jars and lids.

Pickles

The pickles are soft

These should be crunchy. They will be soft if the vegetables were not salted for long enough, or if the salt or vinegar solution was too weak.

The pickles are slippery and soft

Air has got into the pickles through a poor seal and caused spoilage. Or the salt or vinegar solution was not strong enough and bacteria have not been destroyed. **Discard the pickles right away.**

The pickles are dark and/or cloudy

Table salt with iodine and anti-caking agents was used. Or dark vinegar was used. Or too many spices were added. Using soft water or bottled or filtered water can help keep the pickles bright. Hard water can darken pickles. Reactive utensils such as copper or iron were used.

Chutneys, ketchups and salsas

There is mould on the surface

Air and, with it, bacteria has entered the container through an imperfect seal. Do not simply discard the mould and consume the rest of the jar's contents, but **discard the entire jar.** Remember to always use recommended jars and lids, and process in a boiling water bath if keeping salsas and ketchups for any length of time.

It doesn't smell good

Any preserve that has an unpleasant or off-putting smell should be **discarded immediately.**

It appears to be fermenting

Small bubbles appearing round the edges or on the surface indicate that the preserve is fermenting. **This may produce harmful toxins and the product should be discarded right away.** Fermentation can be caused, depending on the type of preserve, by too little sugar, too weak a brine or vinegar solution, inadequate sterilization of equipment, and too warm storage conditions.

Jam Today

And the Quangle Wangle said

To himself on the Crumpetty Tree,

'Jam and jelly and bread,

Are the best of food for me!'

Edward Lear, *The Quangle Wangle's Hat*

Jam

This is a simple preserve of fruit cooked until soft, usually with a little water, when sugar is added and the mixture boiled until setting point is reached, which is when the mixture reaches 105°C/221°F; a sugar thermometer is useful. It is important not to cook the fruit and sugar beyond its setting point, as the sugar will caramelise and the fruit flavour will be much diminished.

In these recipes, I add floral notes, either with fresh flowers, sugar, or syrup, recipes for the last two of which are on p.60.

To test jam and jelly for a set without a thermometer

The mixture will begin to look like jam after about 10 minutes, with a slightly thicker texture and slightly darker appearance than when you started cooking it. The fruit will also become more translucent as it absorbs the sugar. To test, remove the pan from the heat. The setting point is reached when the jam begins to fall off the wooden spoon in a long "curtain" rather than single drops. You can also drop a little on a cold saucer – when the jam or jelly is cold, push it gently with your finger. If it wrinkles, the jam or jelly has reached its setting point and can be potted.

Unless the recipe states otherwise, jams can be kept for at least a year in the pantry, after which they will begin to lose some of their colour, fragrance, and freshness, and may begin to harden. I notice this particularly with jams sealed with cellophane covers; there is less evaporation with rubber and metal seals.

Jelly

As a general rule, pectin-rich fruit will take about 500 g/ 1 lb/ 2 cups sugar to every 500 ml/17 fl oz/2 cups of juice extracted; fruit lower in pectin will need only about 300 g/10 oz/1 cup of sugar to 500 ml/17 fl oz/2 cups of juice. With pectin-rich fruit, such as quince, you can take a second extract. Let the first boiling drip through the jelly bag for about 20 minutes only. Return the fruit pulp to the pan, with half the water initially used, simmer for 30 minutes, and allow to drip for an hour or so. When making jelly it is a good idea to scald or wet the jelly bag before using it. This way it will absorb less of the fruit extract.

Marmalade

Marmalade-making is not difficult, just somewhat time-consuming, so it is worth making plenty of it. All that is required is a large pan, a large measuring cup, and a large weighing bowl on your scales, together with a long-handled spoon, suitable jars and closures – and plenty of patience. Using the easy recipes on pp.74-79, you will be left with the glowing satisfaction of having filled jars and jars for your store cupboard, as well as for presents.

Quantities can never be exact. For example, you might simmer the oranges longer than I do; they might need it if they are less than fresh. Thus, more water will evaporate in cooking them. You might push more pulp through your sieve than I do; that affects overall weight. Your oranges might contain more juice and/or pectin than mine. If, as I sometimes do, you use too small a pan, you will have to let it off the boil occasionally to stop it bubbling over. All this affects cooking time and quantities of sugar and water.

Mincemeat

From medieval to Victorian times, mincemeat was, as its name suggests, made with minced meat, combined with dried fruit and spices, together with candied citrus peel, suet, and fresh fruit, and then baked into large pies. Today's mincemeat bears some resemblance to earlier recipes, with dried fruit and spices, but generally without the minced meat; the richness is provided by suet or other fats. There were so many versions that the cook has more or less a free hand when it comes to this sumptuous preserve.

Home-made mincemeat is a delight and extraordinarily easy to make. Over the years, I have made rich vegetarian mincemeat, which can be every bit as luxurious as the suet version, and à la carte mincemeat, where you make up a basic recipe, and then add extra ingredients each time you want to use it. I have also created a tropical fruit mincemeat, which is not only rich and luxurious, but also suitable for vegetarians, since it uses not suet but grated coconut cream.

The preserving medium in mincemeat is the sugar and the generous helping of a spirit. Mincemeat is usually made in the autumn for use at Christmas, but I have occasionally kept mine from one year to the next. If it appears to have dried out a little, I refresh it with a measure or two of a spirit.

Jam

Plum jam with rose petals and almonds

This homely jam, lifted with the crunch of almonds and the scent of roses, is one of the easiest of all jams to make; plums have plenty of pectin and the jam sets quickly.

Halve the fruit, discard the stones, and cut each piece in half again. Put the plums in a nonreactive saucepan, add the rose petals and water, and simmer until the fruit is tender. Stir in the sugar and, when it has dissolved, boil briskly until setting point is reached. Stir in the almonds. Remove the pan from the heat. Pot the jam in hot, sterilised jars, seal, and label.

Rosewater or essence can be added to the fruit in the absence of fresh flowers.

makes about five 500 g/ 1 lb jars

1.5 kg/3 lb plums
500 ml/17 fl oz/2 cups scented rose petals
250 ml/8 fl oz/1 cup water
1.5 kg/3 lb/6 cups granulated sugar
100 g/4 oz/1 cup flaked or slivered almonds

Raspberry and lavender jam

Raspberry jam is the classic filling for jam tarts and sponge cakes. This version would be perfect for a jelly roll combined with lavender-scented whipped cream or lavender butter cream.

Rinse and drain the fruit and put it in a heavy nonreactive pan with the lavender bundle but without any water. Cook gently until the juices run, then continue cooking the fruit gently until some of the liquid has evaporated and the volume has been reduced by between one quarter and one third. Add the sugar and lemon juice and, when the sugar has dissolved, boil the mixture briskly until setting point is

makes about four 400 g/ 14 oz jars

6-8 lavender heads, tied in muslin
1 kg/2 lb raspberries
1 kg/2 lb/4 cups jam sugar
juice of 1 lemon

reached. Remove the lavender from the pan and the pan from the heat. Pot the jam in hot, sterilised jars, then seal and label them.

Summer pudding jam

As with summer pudding, the secret here is not to use too many black currants because they overpower all else to such a degree that you may as well use all black currants. This jam should be an enticing blend in which each fruit retains its texture and flavour.

I try to make it with one part each of raspberries, red currants, cherries and gooseberries and one part made up of strawberries and black currants – i.e., 20% each raspberries, redcurrants, cherries and gooseberries and 10% each strawberries and black currants – which is what I do for summer pudding, together with the addition of rose petal sugar. With plenty of pectin-rich fruit, the jam will set easily.

Rinse and drain the fruit and put it in a heavy nonreactive pan without any water. Cook gently until the juices run. Add the lemon juice and sugars, and, when the sugar has dissolved, boil the mixture briskly until setting point is reached. Remove the pan from the heat. Pot the jam in hot, sterilised jars, seal, and label.

makes about four 400 g/ 14 oz jars

1 kg/2 lbs summer berry fruit
– see recipe
juice of 2 lemons
750 g/1 ½ lbs/3 cups
preserving sugar
.250 g/8 oz/1 cup rose petal
sugar (p.26)

Rhubarb, pear and clove pink jam

Chop the washed rhubarb into 2.5 cm/1 inch lengths. Peel, core, and slice the pears and put them and the rhubarb in a nonreactive saucepan with the water. Simmer until the fruit is soft and then add the lemon juice, flower petals, and sugar. Cook gently until the sugar has dissolved, then boil briskly until setting point is reached. Remove the pan from the heat and pour the jam into hot sterilised jars. Seal and label.

makes about four 400 g/ 14 oz jars

1 kg/2 lbs rhubarb
6 pears
125 ml/4 fl oz/½ cup water
juice of 2 lemons
4 heaped tablespoons clove
    pink petals
1 kg/2 lbs/4 cups jam sugar

Gooseberry and elderflower jam

Warm scones or hot buttered toast are the perfect companions for this homely, traditional jam, which is extremely easy to make.

Top and tail the gooseberries – a chore, but worth it. Rinse them and put in a nonreactive saucepan with the water, lemon juice and elderflowers. Simmer until the fruit is tender, then stir in the sugar, let it dissolve and boil the mixture rapidly until setting point is reached. Remove the pan from the heat and discard the bundle of elderflowers. Pot the jam in hot, sterilised jars, seal and label.

makes about six 400 g/ 14 oz jars

1.5 kg/3 lbs gooseberries
500 ml/ 17 fl oz/2 cups
    water
juice of 1 lemon
8 elderflower heads, tied in
    muslin
2 kg/4 lbs/8 cups granulated
    sugar

Strawberry and lavender conserve

With slightly less sugar than jam, the conserve has a softer set and more pronounced fruit flavour. It should be stored in the fridge.

Put the strawberries in a bowl, sprinkle on a quarter of the sugar and the lemon juice and leave in a cool place overnight for the juices to draw out of the fruit.

Strain the liquid into a saucepan, add the remaining sugar and the lavender and stir over a gentle heat, without boiling, for about 10 minutes. Add the strawberries, stir, and boil for 20 to 25 minutes, or until setting point has been reached. Remove the pan from the heat and discard the lavender bundle. Spoon the jam into hot, sterilised jars, seal and label.

makes about three 200 g/ 7 oz jars

600 g/1 ¼ lbs strawberries, rinsed and hulled
juice of 1 lemon
1 teaspoon lavender flowers, tied in muslin
400 g/13 oz/2 cups jam sugar

Fresh fig and rose petal jam

Rare and expensive outside the Mediterranean area, figs are usually eaten as a dessert. But if available in abundance, they can, when combined with the haunting scent of roses, be made into the most heavenly jam.

Look for firm unblemished fruit that just yields when you hold it in your hand without pressing. The skin of a perfectly ripe fruit is velvety and soft, rather than taut and satiny. It can be a number of colours from pale green and golden yellow for early summer figs to deep purple for autumn figs, which are those I use when I make fig jam in my Gozo kitchen. It looks and tastes as fresh and bright as strawberry jam. It is

makes about three 400 g/ 14 oz jars

1 kg/2 lbs ripe purple figs
750 g/ 1 ½ lbs/3 cups jam sugar
250 g/8 oz/1 cup rose petal sugar (p.26)

essential to use jam sugar, which contains pectin, as figs contain no pectin. Alternatively, use granulated sugar and powdered or liquid pectin, following the manufacturer's instructions on the label.

Peel and quarter the figs, put them in a bowl, and cover them with the sugar. Leave overnight. Simmer the fig skins in small saucepan with about 200 ml/7 fl oz/1 cup of water for about 15 minutes, strain them and reserve the lovely red juice.

Next day, combine the fruit and sugars with the fig juice in a nonreactive pan and cook gently until the sugar has dissolved. Boil according to the instructions on the sugar packet, until setting point is reached, which may be as little as 4 minutes. Remove the pan from the heat and then pot the jam in sterilised hot jars, seal and label.

Nectarine, rose petal, and almond jam

These smooth-skinned peaches are perhaps the most delicious of all stone fruit, at their best in mid-summer. The flesh is juicy with a noticeable almond flavour and a good balance of sweetness and acidity. The skin and flesh ranges from white to yellowy orange to pinkish red. The white-fleshed varieties are particularly fine.

This delicate jam makes a delightful filling for small tartlets, or can be used to fill a jelly roll.

Peel and core the apples, then tie the peel and cores in a muslin bundle or tea filter. Dice the apple very small. Halve the nectarines and discard the stone. Chop the fruit. There is no

makes about four 400 g/ 14 oz jars

2 tart apples

8 to 10 nectarines, preferably white-fleshed

500 g/1 lb/2 cups granulated or preserving sugar

250 g/8 oz/1 cup rose petal sugar (p.26)

75 g /3 oz/¾ cup slivered almonds

need to remove the skin, as this is soft. Put the apple in a saucepan with about 150 ml/5 fl oz/ 2/3 cup of water. Cook until the fruit is soft and then add the nectarines. Cook until these too are soft and the apple disintegrated.

Strain the juices into a nonreactive saucepan and add the sugar. Heat gently until the sugar has dissolved, boil the syrup for 2 minutes and then add the fruit. Stir well, bring back to the boil, skim any foam from the surface, and then boil until setting point is reached. Stir in the almonds.

Remove the pan from the heat and fill the hot sterilised jars with the jam. Seal the jars, label, and store in a cool dark place.

Strawberry and rose petal jam

This is the jam that might have made me a small fortune. I developed the recipe for afternoon tea during my first guest chef promotion at the Mandarin Oriental in Hong Kong in the 1980s. Guests loved it with my warm scones and clotted cream, and Chef Patissier, Yves Matthey, and I started to make enough to sell in the famous Mandarin Oriental Cake Shop. Yves is still there, overseeing the production of "my" jam, which has been a constant seller ever since, at HKD 258 for a 420 gram jar, over £20. Imagine . . . hundreds of thousands of jars at a modest royalty. Only I never thought to ask for a royalty.

Rinse and hull the fruit, put it in a bowl with the rose petals, cover with the sugar, and add the lemon juice. If you are unable to get rose petals, use rose water instead. Leave overnight. The next day, strain the syrup into a saucepan

makes about three 500 g/ 1 lb jars

750 g/1 ½ lbs strawberries
handful or two of rose petals
750 g/1 ½ lbs/3 cups jam
  sugar
juice of 1 lemon
2 tablespoons rose water –
  optional, see recipe

with 75 ml/3 fl oz/5 tablespoons water, and boil for 5 to 10 minutes. Add the strawberries (and rose petals if using them) and boil until the fruit and syrup jell. Remove the pan from the heat. Spoon the jam into hot, sterilised jars, seal and label.

Cook's tip

Instead of rose water or fresh rose petals, you can also use a couple of tablespoons of dried rose petals (the kind you use for *tisanes*, not *potpourri*, i.e. for culinary use only) and steep them in the 75 ml water that will be used for the syrup, then add the strained petals to the fruit before you cook it.

Mango, jasmine, and lime jam

I like to make this jam in an English winter when, apart from stored apples and pears, only imported fruit is available. Its tropical scents and flavours brighten a cold gray day no end. And if there is slightly more jam than I have jars at the ready, I spoon it through thick yoghurt or over vanilla ice cream for an instant dessert.

Put the sliced limes in the pan with the water and jasmine flowers, and simmer gently until the fruit is soft. Add lime and lemon juice and the mango and cook for 5 minutes. Stir in the sugar and let it dissolve over moderate heat, then bring to the boil, and boil until setting point is reached. Remove the pan from the heat. Ladle the jam into hot sterilised jars, first arranging the lime slices round the sides so that they will be visible, then seal and label.

makes about four 400 g/ 14 oz jars

6 limes, thinly sliced
150 ml/5 fl oz/ ²/₃ cup water
2 tablespoons dried jasmine flowers
juice of 2 limes and 2 lemons
6 large mangoes, peeled and diced
1 kg/2 lbs/4 cups jam sugar

Date and orange flower jam

Just as cucumber sandwiches are for summer, date jam is a lovely winter preserve, especially for tartlets. I also use the date jam as a purée to accompany grilled duck breasts or as a glaze for roast duck or pork.

Put the dates, citrus zest and juice, water, sugar, and aniseed in a saucepan, cook gently until the sugar has dissolved, and allow the mixture to thicken slightly. Remove the pan from the heat. Rub the date mixture through a sieve and add nuts, or seeds, if using them, and stir in the orange flower water. Spoon into small sterilised jars, seal and label for presents, or keep in an airtight container in the fridge. The date jam is also delicious served with yoghurt, ice cream, pancakes and *coeurs à la crème*, the small French cream cheese hearts.

makes about four 200 g/ 7 oz jars

500 g/1 lb dates, stoned and chopped

grated zest and juice of ½ lemon

grated zest and juice of 1 tangerine or bitter (Seville) orange

200 ml/7 fl oz/ ¾ cup water

250 g/8 oz/1 cup light brown sugar

1 to 2 teaspoons aniseed or fennel seeds

2 tablespoons lightly toasted sesame seeds (optional)

2 tablespoons walnuts, chopped (optional)

2 tablespoons lightly toasted flaked almonds (optional)

1 tablespoon orange flower water

Muscat grape and saffron jam

When buying muscat grapes, choose bunches that have turned a pale golden colour for the fullest flavour, rather than buying them green.

Put the saffron in a small bowl, boil the water, pour it on the saffron, and leave to infuse for 20 minutes.

Meanwhile, slit open each grape without cutting right through and put them in a jam pan or suitable saucepan together with the sugar and the saffron liquid. Bring to the boil and cook for 7 minutes, or according to the instructions on the jam sugar pack, until setting point is reached, stirring all the time. Pour into hot sterilised jam jars. Seal and label them and store in a cool dark place.

makes about three 400 g/ 14 oz jars

Pinch of saffron, 15 to 20 threads
125 ml/4 fl oz/½ cup water
1 kg/2 lbs seedless large muscat grapes
1 kg/2 lbs/4 cups jam sugar

Persimmon, mandarin, and orange flower jam

I make this jam around Christmas time, when persimmons reach us from Spain and Italy, and the first of the little Mediterranean "easy peelers" are on the shelves. The jam makes an excellent filling for a jelly roll or a Christmas log, and is equally good spooned into thick Greek yoghurt.

The true persimmon is exceedingly bitter when under-ripe, as it is full of tannin. It becomes soft and translucent as it ripens and looks as swollen as a balloon filled with water. The skin puckers when touched, and the tannins have developed into a mellow sweetness.

The time to buy and use persimmons is when they look so over-ripe that they appear spoiled.

makes about four 400 g/ 14 oz jars

1 kg/2 lbs/4 cups persimmon pulp – see recipe
juice of 2 lemons
6 mandarins
1 kg/2 lbs/4 cups jam sugar
3 tablespoons of orange flower water – see recipe

Because of this, they are often marked down and one can buy them at a fraction of the usual price.

To use the fruit, slit them open and scoop out the sweet fruit pulp into a large measuring cup, and you are ready to make persimmon jam.

Newer hybrids of the fruit have been developed without the tannins, and these can be purchased and used when still firm to the touch. I like to look for fruit with a rich orange glow. The skin of these fruit can be quite tough, so I peel them before chopping the pulp.

Put the fruit pulp in a nonreactive saucepan with the lemon juice, juice of three mandarins, and the well-trimmed segments of the other three, together with the sugar. Cook gently until the sugar has dissolved, add the orange flower water, then boil the mixture until setting point is reached. Remove the pan from the heat. Pot the jam in sterilised hot jars, then seal and label.

Cape gooseberry and jasmine jam

These small golden berries enveloped in a thin, papery husk used to be a winter treat from warmer climates, and I first came across them when I lived in the Cape for a short while as a girl. Now we get them from several countries at different times of the year, but mainly from Colombia. The flavour is similar to that of a soft ripe gooseberry, tart and mildly scented, and with a slightly resinous texture and taste. If you need to keep them for a few days, put them in an airtight box in the fridge.

This is a delicious, if expensive, jam. Use it in pancakes or to flavour creams for cake fillings.

makes about three 200 g/ 7 oz jars

500 g/1 lb Cape gooseberries (physalis), stalks and husks removed

1 tablespoon water

Juice of 1 lemon

1 to 2 tablespoons jasmine flowers, tied in muslin

500 g/1 lb/2 cups granulated sugar

Rinse the fruit well and simmer it, the lemon juice and the jasmine flowers with the water in a nonreactive saucepan until soft, then add the sugar. Cook gently until the sugar has dissolved, then boil briskly until setting point is reached. Remove from the heat, discard the jasmine flowers, and allow the jam to cool slightly. Stir to distribute the fruit evenly, then pot in small, hot sterilised jars, seal, and label.

Blueberry and violet jam

This is a recipe to make if you happen to have a bottle of violet liqueur languishing in your drinks cupboard. Or see p.21.

As well as serving it with the breakfast toast or croissants, blueberry and violet jam is a delicious topping for ice cream, or it can be stirred it into a bowl of plain yoghurt.

Put the fruit in a nonreactive saucepan with the water and simmer until the fruit is soft. Add the sugar and lemon juice and cook gently until the sugar has dissolved, then boil briskly until setting point is almost reached. Stir in the violet liqueur and let the jam reach a set. Remove the pan from the heat and allow the jam to cool slightly. Stir to distribute the fruit evenly, then pot in hot, sterilised jars, seal, and label.

makes about two 400 g/ 14 oz jars

500 g/1 lb blueberries
2 tablespoons water
500 g/1 lb/2 cups preserving
    sugar
Juice of 1 lemon
3 tablespoons violet liqueur

Cherry and carnation jam

As well as its traditional breakfast and teatime uses, cherry and carnation jam makes a perfect filling, with or without whipped cream, for a rich chocolate cake.

Put the sugar and half the raspberry and red currant juice in a saucepan and heat gently until the sugar has dissolved. Add the rest of the juice and pour everything over the cherries in a nonreactive bowl or saucepan. Next day, bring everything to the boil, including the lemon juice and flower petals, and boil rapidly until setting point is reached. Remove the pan from the heat. Discard the bundle of petals. Spoon the jam into steril-ised, hot jars then seal and label.

makes about five 400 g/ 14 oz jars

1.5 kg/6 cups preserving
    sugar (a little less if the
    fruit is very sweet)
125 ml/4 fl oz/½ cup
    raspberry juice
125 ml/4 fl oz/½ cup red
    currant juice, squeezed and
    strained from the fresh fruit
1.5 kg/3 lbs cherries, stoned
Juice of 1 lemon
3 heaping tablespoons
    carnation or clove pink
    petals, tied in muslin

Cook's tip

Strawberry jam can be made in exactly the same way, as, like cherries, they are low in pectin and need the added pectin to be found in redcurrant juice. You can, of course, use jam sugar instead.

Peach Melba jam with a hint of lavender

Fresh peaches and raspberries are two of the ingredients in the classic dish *Pêche Melba*, created by the chef Escoffier in honour of the Australian opera singer, Dame Nellie Melba. The flavours translate beautifully into a jam for high summer, especially with a breath of fresh lavender. Spooned over a scoop of vanilla ice cream in a meringue nest, it makes an instant dessert.

Peel and core the apple and tie the peel and cores in a muslin bundle or tea filter. Dice the

makes about four 400 g/ 14 oz jars

1 tart apple
1 kg/2 lbs peaches, any variety
juice of 2 lemons
750 g/1 ½ lbs/3 cups
    granulated sugar
250 g/8 oz raspberries
1 teaspoon lavender, tied in
    muslin

apple very small. Halve the peaches and discard the stones. Chop the fruit. There is no need to remove the skin as this is soft. Put the apple in a saucepan with the bundle of peel and core and about 150 ml/5 fl oz/$^2/_3$ cup water. Cook until the fruit is soft and then add the peaches. Cook until these too are soft and the apple has completely collapsed into a purée. You can discard the bundle of apple peel and core at this stage.

Strain the juices into a nonreactive saucepan and add the lemon juice and sugar. Heat gently until the sugar has dissolved, boil the syrup for 2 minutes, then add the cooked fruit, the raspberries, and the lavender. Stir well, bring back to the boil, skim any foam from the surface, then boil until setting point is reached. This will take only a few minutes.

Remove the pan from the heat, discard the lavender, and allow the jam to stand for 5 minutes, after which stir to distribute the fruit evenly. Fill hot sterilised jars with the jam. Seal the jars, label and store in a cool dark place.

Guava and jasmine preserve

When I was invited to Colombia as guest cook, guava preserve became one of my favorite tastes, especially for breakfast, where it would appear in warm pastries, to be eaten with cream cheese. Firmer and denser than jelly, but softer than *goiabada* – guava paste – guava preserve is perfect as a filling for cakes, tarts and pastries, with or without cream or cream cheese. When replicating the recipe at home, I found the addition of jasmine only enhanced this tropical delicacy.

makes about four 200 g/ 7 oz jars

500 g/1 lb fresh guavas
2 to 3 heaping tablespoons fresh jasmine flowers, or 1 of dried
Water – see recipe
500 g/1 lb/2 cups jam sugar
Juice of 1 lemon

And then, some time later, I found that using rose petals in place of the jasmine is every bit as good.

Peel and halve the guavas. Scoop out the seeds and put them in a saucepan with the skins, the jasmine flowers and about 200 ml/7 fl oz of water. Simmer for 20 to 30 minutes, then strain the liquid into a larger saucepan. Add the guavas, sliced or cut into chunks, and cook until just soft. Stir in the sugar and lemon juice and, once the sugar has dissolved, boil briskly until setting point is reached, which should not take much more than 4 to 5 minutes when using jam sugar. Remove the pan from the heat. Spoon the preserve into small, hot sterilised jars, seal and label.

Lychee preserves

Many wine tasters liken the scent and flavour of Alsace Gewürztraminer to the lychee, which also has hints of roses in its bouquet, and I have taken this combination to make a delicious preserve, with the whole fruit suspended in the pale jelly. This is a relatively expensive preserve to make, and I serve it as dessert, in small glasses or custard cups.

Generally available in the winter months, the fruit is at its best when the shell is pink rather than brown, and not too pale. Too brown and the fruit will be over-ripe or will have been stored for too long. The brittle, rough shell cracks easily when pressed between thumb and finger, and can be peeled off cleanly to reveal the pearly white fruit inside.

makes about five 400 g/ 14 oz jars

500 ml/17 fl oz/2 cups
    Alsace Gewurztraminer
1.5 kg/3 lbs peeled and
    seeded lychees
750 g/1 ½ lbs/3 cups jam
    sugar
250 g/8 oz/1 cup rose petal
    sugar (p.26)
Juice of 1 lemon

The sweet flesh has a slightly grape-like texture but is denser and delicately scented. Deep within the flesh is a long, shiny, oval, brown, inedible seed; this can be removed by running a sharp knife half-way round the fruit.

Pour half the wine into a saucepan and cook the lychees in it for about 20 minutes. Strain the liquid into another saucepan, add the rest of the wine and bring to the boil. Simmer for a few minutes to evaporate the alcohol, then stir in the sugar, the lemon juice, and the fruit. When the sugar has dissolved, bring to the boil and cook until the mixture reaches jelling point. This may take only 4 or 5 minutes. Follow the instructions on the sugar pack. Remove the pan from the heat. Spoon the preserves into hot sterilised jars, seal and label.

Pineapple, jasmine, and ginger preserve

This is a harmonious combination of flavours, in a preserve which has all the traditional uses and some untraditional ones. A scoop of vanilla ice cream with a spoonful of hot pineapple and ginger preserve is a stunning mixture for an impromptu dessert. And consider brushing some of it over duck or pork, before grilling or roasting, especially if you are combining the meat with oriental flavours.

Peel and thinly slice the ginger, then cut it into matchsticks. Put them in a nonreactive saucepan and cover with water. Simmer until they are almost tender, then add the pineapple chunks and jasmine and 250 ml/8 fl oz/1 cup of water. Simmer for about 10 minutes. Add the lemon juice and sugar and, when the sugar

makes about four 400 g/ 7 oz jars

1 piece of fresh ginger, about 50 g/2 oz
1 large pineapple, peeled, cored and diced, yielding 1 kg/2 lbs/4 cups flesh
2 to 3 heaping tablespoons fresh jasmine flowers or 1 heaping tablespoon dried, tied in muslin
Juice of 2 lemons
1 kg/2 lbs/4 cups jam sugar

has dissolved, raise the heat and boil briskly until setting point is reached. Remove the pan from the heat and discard the bundle of jasmine. Pot the preserve in hot, sterilised jars, and seal and label them.

Apricot and elderflower jam with muscatel wine

This intensely fragrant preserve enhances the muscat scent of elderflowers with a matching dessert wine. A perfect dessert is to use the rich apricot filling in a jelly roll and serve it with a glass of the wine used in the preserve.

Rinse and dry the apricots, halve them and remove their stones, then cut each piece in half again. Put the fruit in a saucepan with the wine and lemon juice and cook until it is soft. Stir in the elderflower syrup and sugar, and, when dissolved, boil briskly until setting point is reached. Remove the pan from the heat and discard the elderflowers. Pot the jam in hot, sterilised jars, seal and label.

makes about six 400 g/ 7 oz jars

1.5 kg/3 lbs ripe apricots
500 ml/17 fl oz/2 cups
    muscatel wine, e.g.
    Beaumes de Venise,
    Moscato d'Asti, Orange
    Muscat
Juice of 1 lemon
250 ml/8 fl oz/1 cup
    elderflower syrup (p.101)
1.25 kg/2 ½ lbs/5 cups jam
    sugar

Rose and apricot jam

I was inspired to make this after tasting Austrian jam made from *Rosenmarillen*, a variety of apricot grown in the Wachau region, noted for its high pectin and acidity. I can find nothing to link the fruit to roses, other than the name, and yet I detected a faint breath of rose perfume when I spread the jam on warm brioche. And this led me to consider combining whatever apricots I could find with rose petals, and more particularly fragrant apricot–coloured roses. With a bit of luck you will find the fruit and flowers come at the same time.

Rinse and dry the apricots, halve them and remove their stones, then cut them in half again. Put the fruit in a saucepan with the rose petals, lemon juice, and water and cook until it is soft. Stir in the sugar and, when dissolved, taste to check whether you need to add a little rosewater, then boil briskly until setting point is reached. Remove the pan from the heat. Pot the jam in hot, sterilised jars, seal and label.

makes about six 400 g/ 7 oz jars

1.5 kg/3 lbs ripe apricots
5 heaping tablespoons scented, apricot-coloured rose petals
Juice of 1 lemon
125 ml/4 fl oz/½ cup water
1.5 kg/3 lbs/6 cups jam sugar
Rosewater – see recipe

Pear, saffron, and walnut jam

This is a lovely combination of autumn flavours, which I use in cakes and tartlets, as well as at teatime.

Boil the water. Put 3 tablespoons of water in a bowl and soak the saffron in it for about 10 minutes.

Put the pears and remaining water in a nonreactive saucepan and simmer until the fruit is soft. Add the lemon juice, walnut pieces, saffron water, and sugar, and cook gently until the sugar has dissolved, then boil briskly until setting point is reached. Remove the pan from the heat, pot in hot, sterilised jars, then seal and label them.

makes about four 400 g/ 14 oz jars

250 ml/8 fl oz/1 cup water
Pinch of saffron, 15 to 20 threads
8 firm pears, peeled, cored, and sliced
Juice of 1 lemon
150 g/5 oz/1 ½ cups walnut pieces
1 kg/2 lbs/4 cups jam sugar

Pumpkin jam with rum, honey, and jasmine

This beautiful golden preserve, with its tropical hints of rum and jasmine, is exquisite spooned over vanilla or rum raisin ice cream.

Cut the pumpkin into manageable pieces and then slice each piece very thinly. Put it in a nonreactive saucepan with the water, jasmine and lemon juice. Cook for 10 minutes, until the pumpkin is just soft, but not collapsing as you want to try to retain the nice thin slices. Add the honey and sugar, stir until the sugar has dissolved, then boil for 5 minutes before adding the rum. Bring back to the boil, cook until setting point has been reached and then remove the pan from the heat. Spoon the jam into hot sterilised jars. Seal the jars and label them.

makes about four 500 g/ 1 lb jars

1.5 kg/3 lbs pumpkin, rind and seeds discarded
1 litre/1 ¾ pint/1 US quart water
2 tablespoons dried jasmine flowers
Juice of 2 lemons
150 g/5 oz/½ cup clear honey
1 kg/2 lbs/4 cups jam sugar
125 ml/4 fl oz/½ cup rum

Christmas jam

Instead of the usual mincemeat for Christmas, one year I used some of the same ingredients to make a Christmas jam. The dried fruit is suspended in apple or quince jelly instead of being bound with suet.

The jam is even more versatile than mincemeat, in that it is delicious on toast, muffins or scones. And you can also use it in tarts and pies – it is especially good when combined with almond paste. If you can get quinces for the jelly, then this is even better, with a more pronounced flavour.

Cut the apples or quinces, without peeling or coring them, in order to retain as much pectin as possible, into chunks. Put them into a large saucepan and simmer in the water until the fruit is soft. Place the chopped dried fruit, including the dates and prunes, in a large bowl and suspend a jelly bag over the bowl. Press the cooked quinces or apples with a potato masher, and then drip the pulp through the jelly bag, preferably overnight.

Next day, put the remaining ingredients, but not the nuts, into a large saucepan and add the soaked dried fruit. Stir well and simmer gently until the sugar has dissolved. Bring to a full boil and boil for 5 minutes. Skim the surface and add the nuts. Boil for 5 minutes or until the mixture jells and remove the pan from the heat. Pot the jam in sterilised hot jars, seal and label.

makes about six 400 g/ 14 oz jars

1.5 kg/3 lbs tart apples or quinces
1.5 litres/3 pints/7.5 cups water
250 g/8 oz/1 ½ cups chopped dried figs
250 g/8 oz/1 ½ cups chopped dried apricots
250 g/8 oz/1 ½ cups chopped dried pears
175 g/6 oz/1 cup chopped stoned dates
175 g/6 oz/1 cup chopped pitted prunes
50 g/2 oz/⅓ cup each candied lemon peel, candied orange peel and undyed glacé cherries
Juice and finely grated zest of 1 orange
Juice and finely grated zest of 1 lemon
½ teaspoon ground cardamom
½ teaspoon ground cinnamon
½ teaspoon ground anise
750 g/1 ½ lbs/3 cups granulated sugar
250 g/8 oz/1 cup rose petal sugar (p.26)
150 g/5 oz/1 ½ cup walnut pieces
150 g/5 oz/1 ½ cup flaked almonds

Savoury jams

There is another type of jam I like to make, a combination of
fruit and vegetable, with a harmonizing floral flavour. Not a
pickle or a chutney, these are sweet, but with a savoury note
from the vegetable, and are made just like a classic jam, but
with a dash of vinegar added. They go very well with cheese
and with meat terrines.

Pineapple, celery, and elderflower jam

Put the pineapple, celery, onion, elderflower
heads, wine, and salt in a nonreactive saucepan
and cook gently until the pineapple and celery
are both soft. Remove from the heat and allow
to cool. Stir in the sugar and vinegar, bring
back to the boil, and cook until setting point
is reached. Remove the pan from the heat and
discard the elderflower heads. Pot the jam in
hot, sterilised jars.

**makes about three 400 g/
14 oz jars**

1 ripe pineapple, peeled, cored,
and diced, yielding about
500 g/1 lb/2 cups flesh
6 celery stalks, trimmed and
sliced
1 mild onion, peeled and
thinly sliced
5 elderflower heads, tied in
muslin
6 tablespoons white wine
½ teaspoon salt
500 g/1 lb/2 cups jam sugar
125 ml/4 fl oz/½ cup white
wine vinegar

Mango, fennel, and fennel flower jam

Put the mangoes, fennel bulbs, onion, fennel flower heads, fennel seeds, wine, and salt in a nonreactive saucepan and cook gently until the fennel is soft. Remove from the heat and allow to cool. Stir in the sugar and vinegar, bring back to the boil, and cook until setting point is reached. Remove the pan from the heat and pot the jam in hot, sterilised jars.

makes about three 400 g/ 14 oz jars

2 ripe but still firm mangoes, peeled and diced
2 large fennel bulbs, trimmed and thinly sliced
1 mild onion, thinly sliced
6 fennel flower heads, tied in muslin
1 teaspoon fennel seeds
6 tablespoons white wine
½ teaspoon salt
500 g/1 lb/2 cups jam sugar
125 ml/4 fl oz/½ cup white wine vinegar

Plum, lavender, and beetroot jam

Peel and dice the beetroot. Halve the plums, discard their stones, cut each piece in half again and put them in a nonreactive saucepan with 2–3 tablespoons water and simmer until the fruit is tender. Add the beetroot to the saucepan. Stir in the wine vinegar, lavender and the sugar, and, when this has dissolved, boil briskly until setting point is reached. Remove the pan from the heat and discard the lavender. Pot the jam in hot, sterilised jars, seal and label.

makes about four 400 g/ 14 oz jars

3 medium beetroot, boiled in the skin until soft
1 kg/2 lbs plums
125 ml/4 fl oz/½ cup red wine vinegar
1 teaspoon lavender flowers, tied in muslin
1 kg/2 lbs/4 cups granulated sugar

Orange, onion, olive, and mint jam

Slice the oranges, remove and discard the peel, and cut each slice in quarters. Put all the ingredients, except for the olives, sugar, and vinegar, in a nonreactive saucepan and cook gently until the onion is soft. Remove from the heat, discard the mint, and allow the mixture to cool. Stir in the olives, sugar, and vinegar. Bring back to the boil and cook until setting point is reached. Remove the pan from the heat and pot the jam in hot, sterilised jars.

makes about three 400 g/ 14 oz jars

6 oranges
3 mild onions, thinly sliced
4 sprigs of fresh mint, tied in muslin
3 tablespoons orange flower water
½ teaspoon salt
8 black olives, stoned and halved
500 g/1 lb/2 cups jam sugar
125 ml/4 fl oz/½ cup white wine vinegar

Tomato, lavender, and shallot jam

Peel and halve the tomatoes and scoop the seeds into a sieve set over a nonreactive saucepan, pushing through as much liquid as possible before discarding them. Put the shallots, lavender, and white wine in the pan. Roughly chop the tomatoes and add with the salt. Cook gently until the shallots are soft, remove from the heat, and allow to cool. Then stir in the sugar and vinegar, bring back to the boil, and cook until setting point is reached. Remove the pan from the heat, discard the lavender, and pot the jam in hot, sterilised jars.

makes about three 400 g/ 14 oz jars

8 large ripe tomatoes
6 banana shallots, peeled and thinly sliced
1 teaspoon lavender flowers, tied in muslin
6 tablespoons white wine
½ teaspoon salt
500 g/1 lb/2 cups jam sugar
125 ml/4 fl oz/½ cup white wine vinegar

Jelly

Quince and rose petal jelly

One of the most beautiful and unusual of all fruits, a ripe quince is always a fruit I long to bite into to experience its haunting flavour and fragrance. Alas, the fruit is inedible raw, but when cooked it delivers a rich, lingering flavour and a deep coral colour, never more evident than in quince jelly. Having a high pectin content, quince jelly sets very easily. It takes happily to many accompanying flavour, but I love it with the scent and flavour of roses. Rosewater or rose essence can be added to the fruit in the absence of fresh flowers, but rose petals suspended in the jelly look very attractive.

Rinse the fruit, but do not peel it, and wipe off the down. Using a sharp and heavy knife, as the fruit is so hard, chop the quinces, including the cores, and put them in a nonreactive pan. Cover with water, add half the rose petals, and simmer until the fruit is soft. This can take more than an hour. Mash the fruit with a potato masher, then spoon it into a jelly bag and let the extract drip for several hours or overnight, if more convenient. Save the pulp for the quince paste recipe on p.94.

Measure the juice and, for each 500 ml/17 fl oz/2 cups, add 500 g/1 lb/2 cups of sugar. Put both in a pan with the remaining rose petals and heat gently until the sugar has dissolved. Boil briskly until setting point is reached and remove the pan from the heat. Spoon the jelly into hot, sterilised jars, and seal and label them.

makes about six 400 g/ 14 oz jars

6 large quinces
Water – see recipe
500 ml/17 fl oz/2 cups scented red rose petals
Granulated or preserving sugar – see recipe

Cook's tip

It is worth keeping back some of the quince extract, once it has dripped through the jelly bag, and freezing it for use with fruit such as strawberries and cherries, which are low in pectin.

Raspberry and lavender jelly

Without seeds, and a truly glorious colour, this lavender-scented raspberry jelly is one of my favourite preserves. Toasted, buttered English muffins are called for. But also try a spoonful run over the top of a white chocolate mousse.

Put the raspberries in a saucepan with a few tablespoons of water. Cook the fruit gently until very soft, then crush it with a potato masher. Spoon the purée into a jelly bag and let it drip for several hours or overnight, if more convenient. Do not squeeze the bag, because if any pulp drips through, it will spoil the clarity of this exquisite jelly.

Measure the liquid and allow 500 g/1 lb/2 cups of sugar to every 500 ml/17 fl oz/2 cups of liquid. Put both in a saucepan, together with the lemon juice and the lavender, heat gently until the sugar has dissolved, and then boil briskly until setting point is reached. Remove the pan from the heat and discard the lavender. Pot the jelly in small, hot, sterilised jars, and seal and label them.

makes about five 200 g/ 7 oz jars

1 kg/2 lbs raspberries
Jam sugar – see recipe
Juice of 1 lemon
1 teaspoon fresh lavender, tied in muslin

Gooseberry and elderflower jelly

With luck, the elder trees come into flower at the same time as the first of the gooseberries are picked. Gooseberries are rich in pectin, which makes them an ideal fruit for jams, chutneys, and jellies. They are comparatively inexpensive and when there is a glut I make them into jelly; not as economical as jam, but I love its pale pink-gold colour. At the beginning of the season I flavour a few jars with elderflowers. Later in the season, with the red fruit, I make a darker, fragrant jelly by infusing lavender heads with the fruit.

When cooking the fruit for jelly-making, there is no need to top and tail, but for any preserve recipe that requires the whole berry, use a sharp knife or scissors to trim them.

The juice from early green gooseberries which drips through the jelly bag has a tartness that makes it an interesting substitute for lemon or lime juices. I use it in salad dressings, marinades, and fish sauces. The jelly is excellent for glazing fruit tarts.

Put the gooseberries in a saucepan with the lemon juice and elderflowers, adding enough water to cover them by 2.5 cm/1 inch or so. Cook until the fruit is soft and mash it to extract as much juice and pectin as possible. Strain through a jelly bag for several hours or overnight.

Measure the volume of the liquid and then an equal volume of sugar. Put in a nonreactive pan, heat the mixture gently, and cook until the sugar has dissolved, then bring to boiling point. Boil fast until setting point is reached and remove the pan from the heat. Pot the jelly in hot, sterilised jars, seal and label.

makes about four 200 g/ 14 oz jars

1.5 kg/3 lbs gooseberries
Juice of 1 lemon
8 to 10 elderflower heads
Granulated sugar – see recipe

Gooseberry, elderflower, and Sauvignon Blanc jelly

Hints of gooseberry and hedgerow flowers are often found in wines made with the Sauvignon Blanc grape. Here I combine the three in a jelly with intriguing flavours. It is excellent for glazing fruit tarts.

Put the gooseberries in a saucepan with the elderflowers, adding enough wine to cover by 2.5cm/1 inch or so. Cook until the fruit is soft. Mash the fruit to extract as much juice and pectin as possible. Strain through a jelly bag for several hours or overnight.

Measure the volume of the liquid, and then an equal volume of sugar. Put in a nonreactive pan. Heat the mixture gently and cook until the sugar has dissolved, then bring to boiling point. Boil fast until setting point is reached and remove the pan from the heat. Pot the jelly in hot, sterilised jars, seal and label.

makes about four 200 g/ 14 oz jars

1.5 kg/3 lbs gooseberries
4 elderflower heads
Sauvignon Blanc – see recipe
Granulated sugar – see recipe

Rose petal and grape jelly

Chop the apples, cores as well, and put in a saucepan. Add enough water to cover them by 2.5cm/1 inch or so. Cook until the apple is almost soft, then add the grapes and cook until they are soft. Mash the fruit to extract as much juice and pectin as possible. Put half the rose petals in a large bowl and set the jelly bag over it. Strain the hot grapes and juice through the jelly bag for several hours or overnight.

Measure the liquid and then measure out an equal volume of sugar. Pound the remaining rose petals in a small quantity of the sugar and mix with the juice and the rest of the sugar.

makes about eight 200 g/ 7 oz jars

2 tart apples such as Granny Smith
1 kg/2 lbs bunch black muscat grapes
Granulated sugar – see recipe
500 ml/17 fl oz/2 cups or more scented, dark red rose petals
1 tablespoon rosewater – if necessary

Put in a preserving pan or heavy saucepan, heat gently, and cook until the sugar has dissolved. Bring the syrup to boiling point. Taste and add the rosewater if you think it necessary. Boil fast until setting point is reached, and then pot in small, clean, hot jam jars. Seal and label.

Rose-scented pomegranate and pink champagne jelly

This prettily coloured jelly makes excellent presents. It is delicious on ice cream or served with pancakes or scones. You can also use it as a glaze for fruit tarts. I have to say that once it is in the jar, pink champagne is not very different from any rosé wine, but it reads well on the label.

Put the pomegranate juice and rose petals in a nonreactive saucepan and bring to the boil. Remove from the heat and leave the petals to infuse until the liquid is cold. Stir in the sugar and return the pan to a gentle heat, until the sugar has dissolved, then add the champagne and lemon juice. Taste, and add the rosewater, if you think it needs it. Bring to the boil and cook until setting point is reached.

Remove the pan from the heat and skim and discard any foam from the surface. Pour the jelly into hot, sterilised jars, seal and label.

makes about five 200 g/ 7 oz jars

500 ml/17 fl oz/2 cups pomegranate juice
2 tablespoons dried rose petals
750 g/1 ½ lbs/3 cups jam sugar
250 ml/8 fl oz/1 cup rosé champagne or other pink sparkling wine
2 teaspoons lemon juice
1 teaspoon rosewater – optional, see recipe

Sloe gin and rose petal jelly

Put the sloes in a nonreactive saucepan with half the rose petals and cover with water. Simmer until the fruit is soft. Crush with a potato masher, then spoon into a jelly bag suspended over a bowl and let the mixture drip onto the remaining rose petals. This can be done and left to stand overnight.

Measure the juice and pour it and an equal volume of sugar into a nonreactive saucepan. Heat gently until the sugar has dissolved and then boil until setting point is reached. Remove the pan from the heat. Pot the jelly immediately in hot, sterilised jars, seal and label.

If you cannot get dried rose petals, use rosewater, adding it with the sugar. Sometimes it is possible to find very late garden roses, in which case you can use fresh petals.

makes three 200 g/7 *oz* jars

500 g/1 lb gin-soaked sloes, left over from making sloe gin – see p.108
2 heaped tablespoons dried, scented rose petals
750 ml/1 ¼ pint/3 cups water – see recipe
Jam sugar – see recipe
1 tablespoon rosewater – see recipe

Crab apple and sage flower jelly

You can also use windfall apples for this recipe, providing they are not too bruised.

This brilliant, clear, jewel-like jelly can be eaten with hot toast or scones, and it also makes an unusual and delicious relish to serve with meat such as roast pork or pheasant.

Put the fruit, water, and half the sage into a nonreactive saucepan and simmer until the fruit is soft. Crush with a potato masher, then spoon into a suspended jelly bag and let the mixture drip through for 20 minutes. Return the pulp to the saucepan and add 250 ml/8 fl oz/1 cup of water. Simmer for 30 minutes

makes about four 400 g/ 14 oz jars

1 kg/2 lbs crab apples
500 ml/17 fl oz/2 cups water
3 or 4 sprigs of sage
1 kg/2 lbs/4 cups preserving sugar
3 tablespoons fresh sage flowers

and once again spoon the pulp into a jelly bag. Let it drip for several hours, without squeezing the bag.

Measure the juice, which should be about 1 litre/1 ¾ pint/4 cups, and pour into a nonreactive saucepan. Add the preserving sugar, the remaining sage, and half the sage flowers. Heat gently until the sugar has dissolved, then boil briskly until setting point is reached. Remove the pan from the heat and stir in the remaining sage flowers. Pot the jelly immediately in hot, sterilised jars, seal and label.

Blackcurrant and violet jelly

Obviously delicious on scones or toast, blackcurrant and violet jelly makes a surprisingly good filling for chocolate cakes. A spoonful or two in hot water makes a soothing drink for sore throats, and is rich in Vitamin C. The violet and blackcurrant combination is also found in one of my favourite macaroons.

Put the fruit and water in a nonreactive saucepan and simmer until the fruit is soft. Crush it with a potato masher before spooning it into a jelly bag and letting it drip into a bowl or jug.

Measure the juice and an equal amount of sugar. Put both in a saucepan and heat gently until the sugar has dissolved. Then boil briskly until setting point is reached. Stir in the liqueur and leave on the boil for a couple of minutes before removing the pan from the heat. Pour the jelly into hot, sterilised jars, seal and label.

makes about three 400 g/ 14 oz jars

1 kg/2 lbs blackcurrants
500 ml/17 fl oz/2 cups water
Granulated sugar – see recipe
3 tablespoons violet liqueur

Fennel, chilli, and hibiscus jelly

Serve this as an accompaniment to roast pork or roast duck, and indeed with sandwiches, wraps, or *fajitas* made with these meats. Or try a spoonful of it with fresh goat cheese or other soft cheese. The bright red hibiscus flowers add a fresh sharp note, rather than a fragrance, and look very striking in the jar. It is worth making enough to give as presents.

Cut the apples into chunks, without peeling or coring them, and put them in a large saucepan, together with one of the chillies, sliced, and the fennel's fronds and chopped outer leaves. Cover with water and simmer until the apples are tender and pulpy. Remove the pan from the heat. Strain the pulp through a jelly bag without squeezing or forcing; otherwise, the jelly will be cloudy.

Meanwhile, halve the rest of the fennel length-wise, then slice it thinly so that each slice has several layers of leaves, just attached at the base.

Measure the strained apple liquid and add 500 g/ 1 lb/2 cups of sugar for each 500 ml/17 fl oz/ 2 cups of liquid. Strain the lemon juice into a saucepan and add the apple extract, sugar, the sliced fennel, and remaining chilli. Bring everything to the boil and cook briskly for 10 minutes or until setting point is reached. Remove the pan from the heat.

Put a hibiscus flower into each sterilised jar, then pour in the jelly, aiming to distribute the fennel and chilli pieces equally. Seal and label the jars.

makes about six 250 g/ 8 oz jars

4 tart green apples
2 red chillies, halved and
   seeds discarded
2 large fennel bulbs
Juice of 2 lemons
Granulated sugar – see recipe
6 hibiscus flowers

Cook's tip

If you can't find hibiscus, a head of fennel flowers can be added to each jar before adding the jelly.

Red currant and clove carnation jelly

This is a savoury jelly, to serve with grilled and roasted meats, especially lamb and game, but also try it brushed over a salmon fillet, just before grilling.

Put the fruit, water, flower petals, and cloves in a nonreactive saucepan and simmer until the fruit is soft. Crush it with a potato masher before spooning it into a jelly bag and letting it drip into a bowl or jug for a few hours or overnight.

Pour in the cider vinegar and measure the liquid. Add an equal volume of sugar, put both in a nonreactive saucepan and heat gently until the sugar has dissolved. Then boil briskly until setting point is reached. Remove the pan from the heat. Pot the jelly into hot, sterilised jars, seal and label.

makes about three 200 g/ 7 oz jars

500 g/1 lb red currants
250 ml/8 fl oz/1 cup water
3 to 4 heaped tablespoons clove pink or carnation petals
½ teaspoon cloves
125 ml/4 fl oz/½ cup cider vinegar
Granulated sugar – see recipe

Scented hedgerow jelly

Use whatever edible wild berries, fruit, hips, and haws you can find, and if possible, use those of the same colour to give red or purple jellies. On the other hand, real foragers will not be too bothered about this nicety and will use a handful of this and a portion of that. Most of these wild fruits are sour and indeed quite inedible unless cooked with sugar, and they have enough pectin to give them a set. Elderberries need added pectin, which is best obtained from windfall apples, cookers, or

makes six 250 g/8 oz jars

1 kg/2 lbs edible hedgerow berries and fruit – see recipe
2 generous handfuls wild rose (Rosa rugosa) petals
Water – see recipe
Granulated sugar – see recipe
Rosewater – see recipe

crabs, or freeze them until you can get the first of the cranberries. Hips, haws, and rowanberries are not very juicy and, again, it is a good plan to cook them with apples to give extra juice.

Do not imagine that you need to be deep in the countryside to hunt for wild food. In Jane Grigson's memorable phrase, you can find rowanberries in "tamed crimplene comfort along suburban avenues." My own London street boasts several rowan trees, a crab apple tree, an elder bush and a nearby blackberry patch. But, as with all wild food, be careful not to pick from bushes that have been blasted with exhaust fumes, and rinse everything thoroughly in warm water.

Cook the fruit and rose petals until soft. The juiciest fruit needs only 2.5 cm/1 inch or so of water in the pan, drier fruit should have about half its volume of water, and the hardest fruit should be almost covered with water. When the fruit is soft, mash it to extract all the pulp and essences. Suspend a jelly bag and let the pulp drip through it overnight. Measure out the juice, and for each 500 ml/17 fl oz/2 cups, measure out an equal volume of sugar. Put both in a saucepan and heat gently until the sugar has dissolved. Taste the syrup and add the rosewater if you think it needs it. Then boil fast until setting point is reached. Pot in small, hot, sterilised jars; seal and label.

Cook's tip

If you have only a small amount of fruit and want to make spiced jelly to serve with game, cook the fruit not with water but with cider vinegar, a stick of cinnamon, a couple of cloves, and few crushed cardamom pods. This is an excellent way of using windfall apples.

Nasturtium and chilli jelly

This vivid and piquant jelly is perfect with soft cheeses and as an accompaniment to grills, and goes splendidly with bangers and mash.

Put all the ingredients in a nonreactive saucepan, heat gently until the sugar has dissolved, and then boil briskly until setting point has been reached. Remove from the heat. Pour the jelly into hot, sterilised jars, aiming to distribute a little chilli and an equal quantity of flowers in each jar. Seal and label.

makes about three 200 g/ 7 oz jars

500 ml/17 fl oz/2 cups apple extract (p.25)
500 ml/17 fl oz/2 cups granulated sugar
15 nasturtium flowers
1 red chilli, thinly sliced
Juice of 1 lime

Elderflower, cucumber, and lemon jelly

Put the lemon zest in a saucepan with the elder-flowers and water. Peel the cucumber and add the skin to the pan, together with the roughly chopped cucumber. Bring to the boil, simmer for 3 or 4 minutes, remove the pan from the heat, cover and leave overnight. Next day, strain the pan's contents through fine muslin or a jelly bag into a measuring cup. Make up to 1 litre/1 ¾ pint/4 cups with a delicate but fairly neutral vinegar, such as cider or white wine vinegar. If you use elderflower vinegar (p.136), as I did

makes six 250 ml/8 oz jars

Zest of 3 lemons
12 to 15 elderflower heads
1 litre/1 ¾ pint/4 cups water
½ cucumber
Vinegar – see recipe
1 kg/2 lbs/4 cups jam sugar

when I first tried this, you may find that the floral flavour predominates, whereas you want a nice balance of cucumber, elderflower and citrus.

Put the liquid and the sugar in a large saucepan, heat gently until the sugar has dissolved, then boil until setting point is reached. Remove from the heat and pot in hot, sterilised jars. Seal and label.

Cook's tip

I devised this recipe to accompany meat dishes, such as chicken and pork, but it is stunning with an oily fish such as salmon, and dresses up smoked mackerel no end. It will also accompany cheese very nicely, from fresh goat cheese to blue cheese.

Wild garlic flower jelly

Wild garlic heralds the beginning of the foraging season for me. I use it in pesto (p.160) and in this clear, savoury jelly, which I like to serve with fresh cheeses, particularly sheep's or goat cheese.

Put the 18 wild garlic flowers and stalks and water in a saucepan. You can roughly chop the stalks. Bring to the boil, simmer for 3 or 4 minutes, remove the pan from the heat, cover, and leave overnight. Next day, strain the pan's contents through fine muslin or a jelly bag into a measuring jug. Makes up to 500 ml/17 fl oz/2 cups with white wine vinegar.

Put the liquid and the sugar in a large saucepan, heat gently until the sugar has dissolved, then boil until setting point is reached. Remove from the heat and pot in hot, sterilised jars, placing a wild garlic flower in each jar. Seal and label.

makes three 250 ml/ 8 oz jars

18 wild garlic flower heads on long stalks
3 wild garlic flower heads on 4cm/1 ½ inch stalks
500 ml/17 fl oz/2 cups water
White wine vinegar – see recipe
500g/1 lb/2 cups jam sugar

Marmalade

Seville orange marmalade with a hint of lavender

Catch them while you can! Unwaxed and otherwise unprocessed, Seville oranges have a limited shelf life so it is worth making the most of the short season for this tricky fruit. Of course, those living in Mediterranean climate zones are lucky enough to have access to bitter oranges for a much longer period.

This marmalade is based on the breakfast classic, which appeals to those who like a preserve with a distinct and tangy personality. When I wrote a regular newspaper column, I quickly realized from readers' letters that there is no such thing as the definitive marmalade recipe; there are as many recipes as there are marmalade-makers. This is the recipe I use in my Gozo kitchen when neighbours bring me bags of oranges and lemons in the winter months.

I feel that one should treat marmalade-making like bread-making, the secret being to make it work to your timetable and not let it master yours.

Rinse and, if necessary, scrub the oranges and lemons, put them in a large nonreactive saucepan, cover with plenty of water, and simmer until the fruit is completely soft; this may take a couple of hours or more. Remove from the heat and allow the fruit to cool. I leave my pot of fruit overnight.

Lift out the oranges and lemons and halve them. Scoop out the pulp and seeds into a sieve set over a bowl. Press as much liquid as you can through the sieve before discarding the pulp and seeds. Finely slice the skins of the orange halves, or

makes about eight 400 g/ 14 oz jars

8 to 10 Seville oranges
2 lemons
Water – see recipe
Granulated sugar – see recipe
1 teaspoon lavender, tied in muslin

process for a few seconds in the food processor. Add the peel to the sieved mixture and weigh.

For every 500 g/1 lb/2 cups of peel and sieved pulp, stir in 500 ml/17 fl oz/2 cups of the cooking liquid, making up the quantity if necessary with water or lemon juice, or a little of both. Weigh it again.

For every 500 g/1 lb/2 cups of this mixture, add 625 g/1 ¼ lbs/2 ½ cups of sugar and put everything in a large nonreactive saucepan with the lavender. Heat gently and, when the sugar has dissolved, bring to the boil and continue cooking until setting point is reached; about half an hour at full boil will usually do it. Remove the pan from the heat.

Allow the marmalade to stand for 15 minutes then discard the lavender bundle and stir to distribute the peel evenly. Fill hot, sterilised jars right to the top, and seal and label.

Peach, lavender, and orange marmalade

A fine combination of tangy citrus and mellow peach, with a breath of lavender, makes this suitable for both breakfast and teatime.

Halve the citrus fruit, squeeze the juice into a jug, and tie any pips in a piece of muslin or a tea filter. Finely shred the citrus peel and put it in a bowl. Add water to the citrus juice to make up to 1 litre/1 ¾ pint/4 cups and pour over the peel. Leave overnight to soften.

Next day, put the soaked peel and liquid in a nonreactive saucepan and simmer for about an hour, by which time the peel will be quite tender. Halve the peaches, discard the stones,

makes about four 400 g/ 14 oz jars

3 sweet oranges

1 lemon

Water – see recipe

6 peaches

Jam sugar – see recipe

1 teaspoon lavender, tied in muslin

500 g/1 lb/2 cups granulated sugar

250 g/8 oz/1 cup rose petal sugar (p.26)

1 tonka bean

chop the fruit and add to the saucepan. Simmer for 10 to 15 minutes until the peaches are soft.

Measure the liquid and fruit, and for each 500 ml/17 fl oz/2 cups, allow 500 g/1 lb/2 cups of sugar. Put the fruit and liquid in a nonreactive saucepan with the lavender, bring to the boil, stir in the sugar, dissolve, and cook briskly until setting point is reached. Remove the pan from the heat and discard the lavender bundle. Pot the marmalade in hot, sterilised jars, then seal and label them.

Scented Christmas marmalade

By Christmas I have usually run out of Seville orange marmalade, so I turn to seasonal mandarins or other small oranges, combined with other citrus fruit, to make a well-flavoured, well-set marmalade scented with a hint of rose and tonka bean.

This is a very flexible recipe; you can use grapefruit skins left over from the breakfast table and orange juice, or, as I do here, mandarin skins left over from a fruit salad.

Cover the mandarin peels with water and simmer until soft. Also add the lemon peels, once you have squeezed and retained the juice. The membranes inside the lemons and any pips should be wrapped in a muslin parcel, together with any seeds from the mandarins, and simmered with the fruit peels.

Once the peels are very soft, finely chop, slice or briefly process and then put them back in a pan with the grapefruit juice and cooking liquid, and reheat.

makes about four 400 g/ 14 oz jars

Peels of 12 mandarin oranges and 3 lemons

500 ml/17 fl oz/2 cups freshly squeezed pink grapefruit juice

500 g/1 lb/2 cups granulated sugar

250 g/8 oz/1 cup rose petal sugar (p.26)

1 tonka bean

When hot, stir in the sugar and, when this has dissolved, boil briskly until the mixture jells. Remove the pan from the heat and leave for a few minutes before grating the tonka bean into the marmalade. Stir to distribute the fruit and pot in sterilised hot jars, seal and label.

Cook's tip

Like a large, dark, wrinkled almond in shape and appearance, the tonka bean, grown in tropical rainforests, has the most beguiling scent and flavour, with hints of vanilla, almond and sweet spices, which, together with what seems like a myriad fragrant volatile oils, are released when the bean is grated or chopped.

Grapefruit and jasmine marmalade

Perfect for those who prefer a sharper, more sophisticated flavour at teatime, this marmalade is also a delight for a leisurely breakfast. And as grapefruit is available year-round, fresh jasmine flowers can be used to make this marmalade in the summer months.

Scrub the fruit well and put it and one of the jasmine bundles in a lidded saucepan with enough water to cover. Cook gently, covered, for 2 hours or until soft. Remove from the heat and allow to cool, overnight if this is convenient.

Discard the jasmine bundle. Halve the fruit and scoop out the pulp and pips into a sieve set over a wide pan. Rub through and add the cooking liquid. Weigh this. Finely slice the grapefruit peel, or process for a few seconds in the food processor and weigh the fruit. Add these two quantities together then weigh out the same amount of sugar. Heat the sugar and liquid

makes about three 400 g/ 14 oz jars

2 large grapefruits
3 tablespoons heaped jasmine flowers, tied in two separate muslin squares
Water – see recipe
Granulated sugar – see recipe

gently and, when the sugar has dissolved, add the second helping of jasmine and boil for a few minutes. Stir the sliced grapefruit peel into the boiling sugar syrup. Continue cooking just until the marmalade reaches setting point. Remove the pan from the heat and allow to stand for 5 minutes to distribute the peel evenly. Remove the jasmine bundle. Pot the marmalade in hot, sterilised jars, seal and label.

Pear and orange marmalade

For a mellower version of the traditional breakfast marmalade, I have used pears, which round out the flavour and produce a velvet-textured preserve. Use sweet or bitter oranges, according to availability, but remember that a thick-skinned orange will produce a more bitter preserve than a thin-skinned one.

Put all the ingredients in a large nonreactive saucepan, bring to the boil over a medium heat, stirring until the sugar has dissolved, and then boil for about 20 minutes until setting point is reached. Remove the pan from the heat. Skim any foam from the surface. Ladle the marmalade into hot, sterilised jars, seal and label.

makes about eight 200 g/ 7 oz jars

12 pears, peeled, cored, and sliced or diced

3 oranges, quartered and thinly sliced, then pre-cooked for 45 to 60 minutes

750 g/1 ½ lbs/3 cups jam sugar

500 g/1 lb/2 cups granulated sugar

2 tablespoons lemon juice

2 tablespoons orange flower water

Sweet fennel and onion marmalade

This is delicious served as part of a mezze or hors d'oeuvres, with, for example, sardines, hard-boiled eggs and olives.

Gently fry the onion in oil for 10 to 15 minutes and then add the fennel, fennel flowers, wine, and spices. Continue cooking for 15 to 20 minutes, stirring from time

makes about five 200 g/ 7 oz jars

4 large mild onions, thinly sliced

6 tablespoons extra virgin olive oil

3 large, round fennel bulbs, sliced

to time to prevent sticking. Add the salt and pepper, and stir in the fruit, nuts, and vinegar. Bring to the boil and cook briskly for 5 minutes, ensuring that the vegetables are quite soft before adding the sugar. Then cook until the mixture has a soft consistency and the vinegar and cooking juices have been absorbed. Remove the pan from the heat, discard the fennel flower bundle, and pot the marmalade in hot, sterilised jars. Seal and label the jars and keep in the fridge or, for longer keeping, heat process following the instructions on p.33.

8 fennel flower heads, tied in muslin
6 tablespoons white wine
1 teaspoon ground cumin
1 teaspoon ground coriander
1 teaspoon salt
1 teaspoon freshly ground black pepper
3 tablespoons sultanas or raisins
3 tablespoons toasted pine nuts or flaked almonds
250 ml/8 fl oz/1 cup white wine vinegar
250 g/8 oz/1 cup granulated sugar

Mincemeat

A la carte floral mincemeat

Choosing the extra ingredients from the list below the basic recipe allows you to vary the intrinsic flavours of the mincemeat.

Chop or mince the dried fruit and then mix all the ingredients in a bowl. Cover and let sit for 24 hours, then pot in sterilised jars, seal and label.

When you wish to use the mincemeat, spoon out about 250 g/8 oz/1 ½ cups into a bowl. That, together with one of the following, will fill 12 to 18 mince pies:

1 tart apple, peeled, cored and grated, and mixed with 75 g/3 oz/¼ cup flaked almonds

1 pear, peeled, cored and grated, and mixed with 1 tablespoon freshly grated ginger, or crystalized ginger

makes about four 500 g/ 1 lb jars

250 g/8 oz/1 ½ cups chopped dried apricots or pitted prunes
250 g/8 oz/1 ½ cups raisins
250 g/8 oz/1 ½ cups chopped dates
250 g/8 oz/1 ½ cups sultanas
250 g/8 oz/1 ½ cups currants
200 g/7 oz/1 cup shredded beef or vegetarian suet OR
125 ml/4 fl oz/½ cup extra virgin rape seed oil OR
200 g/7 oz/1 cup grated coconut cream

1 tart apple mixed with a handful or two of dried cranberries, cherries, or blueberries

Half a medium pineapple, peeled, cored, and chopped, mixed with a handful of pine nuts, finely chopped Brazil nuts, or desiccated coconut

1 fresh mango, peeled and chopped, mixed with a handful of chopped cashew nuts

100 g/4 oz fresh or frozen cranberries, cooked in a little orange juice until they pop, and mixed with chopped mandarin segments and grated zest or chopped kumquats

150 g/5 oz/1 cup light brown sugar OR rose petal sugar OR lavender sugar (pp.25–27)

100 g/4 oz/1 cup chopped mixed peel

Grated zest and juice of 1 lemon

Grated zest and juice of 1 orange

1 tablespoon orange flower water OR rosewater OR a few drops of culinary lavender essence

1 teaspoon ground mixed spice

½ teaspoon ground cardamom

125 ml/4 fl oz/½ cup rum or brandy

125 ml/4 fl oz/½ cup sweet sherry or port

Cornish fig, apple, and rose mincemeat

This is based on a recipe I made when filming a Christmas TV series in Cornwall. When the carol singers and hand-bell ringers came calling for their "figgy pudding," I gave them mince pies, made from this deliciously rich-tasting mincemeat. It will keep very well, since fresh apple is only added when you want to make the mince pies. One peeled, cored, and grated apple is sufficient for 2 jars of mincemeat.

Remove the stalk ends of the figs and roughly chop them and the apples. Put them and the vine fruit in the food processor and process to the texture you prefer.

makes about five 400 g/ 14 oz jars

500 g/1 lb dried figs

500 g/ 1 lb dried apples (not apple crisps, but the leathery rings of dried fruit)

500 g/1 lb/3 cups mixed vine fruit

4 heaping tablespoons candied peel, chopped

150 g/5 oz/1 ½ cups chopped walnuts or almonds

250 g/8 oz/1 cup rose petal sugar (p.26)

Transfer the mixture to a bowl and stir in the rest of the ingredients. Leave overnight for the flavours to blend, then spoon into sterilised jars, cover, seal and label. When you want to use the mincemeat, transfer it to a bowl and stir in the freshly grated apple as described above.

125 ml/4 fl oz/½ cup Somerset cider brandy or Calvados

1 tablespoon rosewater

150 g/5 oz/1 ½ cups vegetarian suet, or coarsely grated, chilled, creamed coconut

1 teaspoon ground cinnamon

1 teaspoon dried rose petals

Pineapple, rum, and jasmine mincemeat

As I make this with creamed coconut instead of suet, the mincemeat is suitable for vegetarians. You can, of course, also use vegetarian suet.

Use this for a mincemeat tart and serve it with rum raisin or jasmine ice cream as an alternative to Christmas pudding. Dried pineapple is available from health food stores and supermarkets, and it can be combined with fresh pineapple and other tropical fruits, both fresh and dried, in this luscious and luxurious mincemeat, which I feel sure our great grandmothers would have loved, if they had had access to all the fabulous dried fruit we can find now.

Scrub the lime or lemon, grate the rind and squeeze the juice into a bowl. Thoroughly mix in the rest of the ingredients and leave overnight for the flavours to blend. Then pot in sterilised jars, seal and label.

makes five 200 g/7 oz jars

1 lime or lemon

200 g/7 oz/1 cup light brown sugar

4 tablespoons jasmine syrup – see p.101

500 g/1 lb dried fruit chosen from the following and chopped small: pineapple, mango, papaya, banana and dates

250 g/8 oz fresh fruit, finely chopped, chosen from the following: pineapple, physalis, guava or mango

200 g/7 oz/1 cup creamed coconut, grated

50 g/2 oz/¼ cup chopped blanched almonds

1 tablespoon dried jasmine flowers

½ teaspoon ground cardamom

½ teaspoon ground cinnamon

½ teaspoon ground mace

2 to 3 tablespoons light rum

Spread a little sunshine

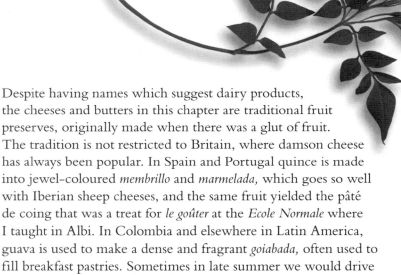

Despite having names which suggest dairy products,
the cheeses and butters in this chapter are traditional fruit
preserves, originally made when there was a glut of fruit.
The tradition is not restricted to Britain, where damson cheese
has always been popular. In Spain and Portugal quince is made
into jewel-coloured *membrillo* and *marmelada,* which goes so well
with Iberian sheep cheeses, and the same fruit yielded the pâté
de coing that was a treat for *le goûter* at the *Ecole Normale* where
I taught in Albi. In Colombia and elsewhere in Latin America,
guava is used to make a dense and fragrant *goiabada,* often used to
fill breakfast pastries. Sometimes in late summer we would drive
through the orchards of Pennsylvania Dutch country where we
would smell the apple butter cooking on small family farms.

A large quantity of fruit is needed for a relatively small yield, as
the fruit pulp is cooked with sugar until it acquires the consistency of heavy cream – for fruit butter – and a very stiff paste
for fruit cheese. The latter is potted in small sterilised jars and
kept for at least 3 to 4 months for the flavours to develop, while
fruit butter is potted as for jam. I add a hint of flowers, either
with floral sugar or floral essence, sometimes with fresh flower
petals if the seasons allow.

Fruit leathers are an even more concentrated form of fruit
preserve. Cooked with sugar to a thick paste, the fruit is

spread out on wax paper or cling film, covered with another sheet and rolled very thin and then dried. Although it originated in the Middle East, probably first made from apricots, it is now also produced commercially in Australia, in the United States, in South Africa, where peach fruit leather is very popular, and other fruit-producing countries. Grapes, plums, blueberries can all be made into this unusual preserve. To use, it was traditionally soaked and reconstituted. Now it is eaten on its own as a high energy snack, and often described as fruit roll-ups.

Extremely rich and luscious, fruit and floral curds are something of a luxury. The essential ingredient is a sharp, acidic fruit, to act as a foil to the suave, velvety blend of eggs, butter, and sugar. Seville oranges, limes, grapefruit, and passion fruit are perfect, especially when paired with a matching floral ingredient. Gooseberry and elderflower curd works if you use the tart green early gooseberries, rather than dessert gooseberries. As for raspberries, strawberries, and even blood oranges, all of which I have seen in curd recipes, I find they are they are too bland to provide a contrast; there are many other better uses for the fruit.

The essential part of the method is the continuous stirring over gentle heat, ensuring that the mixture does not curdle. A *bain-marie*, double boiler, or water bath is the answer. Doing this in a bowl set over a saucepan of water and stirring with a wooden spoon can take 45 minutes or so. But if you set a small stainless steel saucepan inside a larger saucepan of water and use an electric stick blender, the whole process will take less than 10 minutes.

Because, unlike jam, it is not made for long storage at ambient temperature, I prefer to pot curd in small (250 g/8 oz or even smaller) jars, or to keep the curd in an airtight plastic container in the fridge. The curd also freezes very well. I do this in a large ice cube tray, after which I store the frozen cubes in a freezer bag. Fresh curd does not keep long, no more than four weeks, and it must be kept in the coldest part of the fridge.

Important note

The freshest possible eggs should be used, but even though the curds undergo some heat treatment, this is not enough to kill bacteria, and the eggs should be regarded as being raw. **Therefore the usual warnings about consumption of raw eggs apply; pregnant women, the very old, the very young and anyone with immunity deficiency should not consume any of the curds.**

Seville orange curd

As well as the more traditional breakfast and teatime uses, you can also use the curd to make a number of easy, yet luxurious chilled or iced puddings, such as iced soufflés, parfaits, and ice creams.

The orange flower water adds a hint of Andalusia, of which I am always reminded when I use Seville oranges in their short winter season.

Grate the zest from the oranges and rub the sugar cubes firmly over the skin to get any last drops of essential fragrant orange oil. Halve and squeeze the oranges. Beat the eggs and orange flower water together until well beaten. Sieve this into a bowl. Put the zest, sugar cubes, and juice in a double boiler or in a stainless steel saucepan set inside a larger saucepan half-filled with simmering water. Add the eggs, butter, and sugar, and stir until the sugar has dissolved. Continue cooking gently and stir until the mixture thickens. Remove the pan from the heat. Spoon the curd into warm, sterilised jars, cover and seal immediately. Label, refrigerate, and use within 4 weeks.

fills two 250 ml/8 oz jars

3 Seville oranges
2 to 3 sugar cubes/175 g/
    6 oz/¾ cup caster sugar
125 g/4 oz/1 stick unsalted
    butter, cut into pieces
4 eggs
1 tablespoon orange flower
    water

Grapefruit and lavender curd

The curd is delicious served with vanilla ice cream or as a filling for tartlets. You can also stir it into slightly softened vanilla ice cream and freeze it briefly before serving.

Grate the zest and squeeze the juice from the grapefruits, and put in a double boiler or in a stainless steel saucepan set inside a larger saucepan half-filled with simmering water over a low heat. Lightly beat the egg yolks and eggs together. Add them to the pot along with the butter and sugar. Stir until the sugar has dissolved. Continue cooking and stirring until the mixture thickens, 30 to 45 minutes. Remove from the heat. Pot the curd in small, sterilised jars and cover immediately. Label, refrigerate, and use within 4 weeks. Alternatively, freeze the mixture in small containers.

fills four 250 ml/8 oz jars

4 grapefruits with
   unblemished skins
2 egg yolks
4 whole eggs
250 g/8 oz/2 sticks unsalted
   butter, cut into small cubes
375 g/12 oz/1 ½ cups caster
   sugar
125 g/4 oz/½ cup lavender
   sugar (p.26)

Lemon and lavender curd

As well as being delicious on freshly baked scones, this curd is also perfect for a classic lemon tart. Spoon into baked pastry cases and put into a preheated oven at 180°C/350°F/gas mark 4 for 5 to 10 minutes. Serve warm, dusted with powdered sugar immediately before serving.

Grate the zest and squeeze the juice from the lemons, and put in a double boiler or in a stainless steel saucepan, set inside a larger saucepan half-filled with simmering water. Lightly beat the egg yolks and eggs together. Add them to the pot along with the butter and sugar. Stir until the sugar has dissolved.

fills four 250 ml/8 oz jars

4 large lemons with
   unblemished skins
2 egg yolks
4 whole eggs
250 g/8 oz/2 sticks unsalted
   butter, cut into small cubes
250 g/8 oz/1 cup caster
   sugar
250 g/8 oz/1 cup lavender
   sugar (p.26)

Continue cooking gently and stir until the mixture thickens. Remove the pan from the heat. Spoon the curd into warm, sterilised jars, cover, and seal immediately. Label, refrigerate, and use within 4 weeks.

Cook's tip

One of the best ice creams I have ever tasted is made by mixing a pot of lemon and lavender curd with a carton of cream and freezing it. Before it is completely frozen, stir the mixture thoroughly, then carefully fold in some broken meringues and finish the freezing in a container in the freezer, not in the ice cream machine or it will churn the meringue to crumbs, when you want to retain enough texture for the ice cream to crunch when you eat it, for there you have lemon meringue ice cream.

Blackcurrant and lavender curd

My rule of thumb for making curds is to use only fruit with which I would make a posset or a fool, that is, an acid fruit. The tartness and intense flavour of blackcurrants is a perfect foil for the eggs, butter, and sugar, and the fruit and flowers are in season at the same time. You may well not need the additional acidity of the lemon juice. Taste the fruit once you have cooked and sieved it.

Rinse the blackcurrants and put them in a saucepan with a couple of tablespoons of water and the lavender flowers. Cook over gentle heat until the fruit is soft. Discard the lavender bundle and rub the fruit through a sieve into a bowl. Measure out 250 ml/ 8 fl oz/1 cup of purée into a double boiler or a stainless steel saucepan set over a larger saucepan of simmering water. Stir in the

fills four 250 ml/8 oz jars

1kg/2 lbs blackcurrants
1 teaspoon fresh lavender flowers tied in muslin
Juice of half a lemon – see recipe
250 g/8 oz/1 cup caster sugar
2 egg yolks
4 whole eggs
250 g/ 8 oz/2 sticks unsalted butter, cut into small cubes

lemon juice and sugar, and then the eggs and butter. Cook until the mixture thickens sufficiently to coat the back of a spoon. Remove the pan from the heat. Pot the curd in warm sterilised jars, then seal and label. Refrigerate and use within 4 weeks.

Cook's tip

Any remaining curd can be stirred into custard for a perfect blackcurrant fool. Or fill small, crisp tart cases with the fruit and flower purée and top with whipped cream for another speedy dessert.

Loquat and elderflower curd

These small Mediterranean fruits are quite fragile and their pale orange skin often looks spotted with brown bruises. Their flavour is slightly astringent, with a resinous hint, not unlike a mango. They come from a beautiful tree with dark green leaves and are only about 3 cm/1 ½ inch long, with waxy-looking skin, soft apricot-coloured flesh, and a large inedible pit. Their season usually coincides with my making elderflower syrup.

For an instant dessert, spoon some loquat curd into individual meringue shells and top with lightly toasted flaked almonds.

Rinse the loquats, removing any damaged parts, and halve them to remove the pits. Cook gently until soft in the elderflower syrup. Rub through a sieve into a double boiler, *bain-marie* or a stainless steel saucepan set over a larger saucepan of simmering water. Lightly beat the egg yolks and eggs together. Stir the lemon juice and sugar, and then the

fills three 250 ml/8 oz jars

500 g/1 lb loquats
3 tablespoons elderflower
    syrup (p.99)
Juice of 1 lemon
125 g/4 oz /½ cup caster
    sugar
2 egg yolks
4 whole eggs
250 g/8 oz/2 sticks unsalted
    butter, cut into small cubes

eggs and butter into the double boiler. Cook over a gentle heat until the mixture thickens sufficiently to coat the back of a spoon. Remove the pan from the heat. Pot the curd in warm sterilised jars, then seal and label. Refrigerate and use within 4 weeks.

Gooseberry and elderflower curd

It is worth making more gooseberry purée than you need, as the extra makes a delicious gooseberry fool for an instant dessert. Mix it with custard, yogurt, or *crème fraîche,* swirling it together, but not overmixing, spoon it into glasses and serve with a crisp biscuit and lightly toasted flaked almonds.

Rinse the gooseberries and put them in a saucepan with about 1 cm/½ inch of water in the bottom. Add the elderflowers and cook gently until the fruit is soft. Rub through a sieve into a bowl. Measure out 250 ml/8 fl oz/1 cup into a double boiler, *bain-marie* or a stainless steel saucepan set over a larger saucepan of simmering water. Lightly beat the egg yolks and eggs together. Stir the lemon juice and sugar, and then the eggs and butter into the double boiler. Cook over a gentle heat until the mixture thickens sufficiently to coat the back of a spoon and then remove the pan from the heat. Pot the curd in warm sterilised jars, then seal and label. Refrigerate and use within 4 weeks.

Cook's tip

If you don't have fresh elderflowers, cook the gooseberries in elderflower syrup as in the loquat curd recipe (p.87). If you do this, reduce the amount of sugar by about one third.

fills four 250 ml/8 oz jars

1 kg/2 lbs tart green
  gooseberries
4 or 5 elderflower heads
Juice of ½ lemon
250 g/8 oz/1 cup caster sugar
2 egg yolks
4 whole eggs
250 g/8 oz/2 sticks unsalted
  butter, cut into small cubes

Apricot and carnation curd

Although not the tartest of fruit, apricots do have a pronounced acidity and a huge amount of flavour and colour, which makes them a perfect ingredient for fruit butters, curds, and cheeses.

Rinse the apricots, halve them, discard the pits and put them in a saucepan with about 1 cm/½ inch of water in the bottom. Add the flower petals and cloves, and cook gently until the fruit is soft. Rub through a sieve into a bowl. Measure out 250 ml/8 fl oz/1 cup into a double boiler, *bain-marie* or a stainless steel saucepan set over a larger saucepan of simmering water. Lightly beat the egg yolks and eggs together. Stir the lemon juice and sugar, and then the eggs and butter into the double boiler. Cook over a gentle heat until the mixture thickens sufficiently to coat the back of a spoon. Remove the pan from the heat. Pot the curd in warm sterilised jars, then seal and label. Refrigerate and use within 4 weeks.

fills four 250 ml/8 oz jars

20 firm but just ripe apricots
Petals of 8 to 10 clove pinks
  or carnations
2 or 3 cloves
Juice of 1 lemon
250 g/8 oz/1 cup caster sugar
2 egg yolks
4 whole eggs
250 g/8 oz/2 sticks unsalted
  butter, cut into small cubes

Cook's tip

As in previous recipes, any leftover apricot pulp can be used as the base for a fruit fool or ice cream.

Passion fruit and jasmine curd

As a filling for sponge cakes and jelly rolls, and as a dessert when combined with meringues and cream or ice cream, this subtly flavoured curd has no equal. It is worth mastering the craft of making curd just so that you can make this delectable sweet.

It is not true that the more wrinkled a passion fruit is the better; it is just older, and therefore less juicy. The leathery brownish-purple skin encloses a thin reddish pith surrounding a white membranous lining which encloses small edible crunchy seeds, each one set in a fragrant, intensely flavoured, sweet-sour and translucent pulp, dark greenish-orange in colour.

To obtain the sweet pulp, cut the top off the fruit like an egg and spoon out the interior. Both pulp and seeds are edible.

Scoop the pulp from the passion fruit as described above and mix with a tablespoon of boiling water to loosen the pulp and seeds. Rub the pulp through a fine sieve into a double boiler or stainless steel saucepan. Halve and squeeze the lemon and add the juice to the passion fruit pulp together with the jasmine syrup. Put the saucepan inside a larger saucepan half-filled with simmering water. Add the eggs, butter, and sugar and stir until the sugar has dissolved. Mix with an electric stick blender and it will thicken in about 10 minutes. Remove the pan from the heat. Spoon the curd into warm, sterilised jars, cover and seal immediately. Label, refrigerate, and use within 4 weeks.

fills two 250 ml/8 oz jars

4 smooth passion fruits
1 lemon
4 tablespoons jasmine syrup
    – see p.98 for the basic
    flower syrup recipe
2 egg yolks plus 2 whole
    eggs, well beaten and
    strained through a sieve
175g/6 oz/1 ½ sticks unsalted
    butter, cut into pieces
125 g/4 oz/½ cup caster
    sugar

Orange and apricot butter

Not a butter, of course, but a luxurious fruit spread, which you can serve with hot buttered toast, or use as a filling for crêpes or as a sauce for desserts and ice cream.

Soak the apricots in the water overnight and the next day, put them and the cut-up orange into a nonreactive saucepan and simmer until the fruit is soft. Rub the mixture through a sieve. Put the pulp, sugar, and orange flower water in a nonreactive saucepan and simmer until the sugar has dissolved, stirring occasionally. Boil the mixture until thick enough to coat the back of a spoon, and stir from time to time to prevent the mixture from sticking.

Remove the pan from the heat and spoon the fruit butter into hot, sterilised jars. Seal and label the jars and, when cool, refrigerate. It will keep for 2 to 3 months in the fridge. For longer storage in the pantry, process the jars in a water bath, using the method on p. 33.

fills three 250 ml/8 oz jars

500g/1 lb/2 cups dried
  apricots, coarsely chopped
500 ml/17 fl oz/2 cups water
2 thin-skinned oranges, thinly
  sliced and quartered
750 g/1 ½ lbs/3 cups
  granulated sugar
2 tablespoons orange flower
  water

Rose and cardamom-scented apple and pear butter

Although traditionally made with apples, I like to use a combination of apples and pears for a richer, more complex flavour. Try serving it warm, perhaps with a dash of Calvados or *Poire Williams*, over vanilla ice cream.

Put the apples and pears and both juices in a nonreactive saucepan, together with the cardamom seeds. Simmer for about an hour, until the fruit is tender. Blend the fruit with an electric stick blender until smooth, or rub it through a sieve into another nonreactive saucepan. Stir in the sugar. When the sugar has dissolved in the hot mixture, simmer until the mixture thickens, about 40 minutes. Remove the pan from the heat and fill hot, sterilised jars with the butter. Seal and label the jars and, when cool, refrigerate. It will keep for 2 to 3 months in the fridge. For longer storage, process the jars in a boiling water bath, using the method on p.33.

fills eight 250 ml/8 oz jars

8 tart apples, such as Granny Smith, peeled, cored, and chopped
8 pears, such as Bartlett or Seckel, peeled, cored, and chopped
250 ml/8 fl oz/1 cup apple juice
250 ml/8 fl oz/1 cup pear juice
Seeds of 4 cardamom pods
500 g/1 lb/2 cups granulated sugar
250 g/8 oz/1 cup rose petal sugar (p.26)

Peach, jasmine, and almond butter

The addition of ground almonds gives more substance to this floral fruit butter, which makes a delicious filling for fruit tartlets.

Simmer the peaches, jasmine, and water until soft. Rub the mixture through a sieve. Put the pulp, sugar, and lemon juice in a nonreactive saucepan and simmer until the sugar has dissolved, stirring occasionally. Boil the mixture until thick enough to coat the back of a spoon, and stir from time to time to prevent the mixture from sticking. Stir in the almond liqueur and ground almonds. Remove the

fills three 250 ml/8 oz jars

1 kg/2 lbs/4 cups chopped peaches
125 ml/4 fl oz/½ cup water
4-5 heaped tablespoons jasmine flowers
750 ml/1 ¼ pint/3 cups sugar
2 tablespoons lemon juice
1 teaspoon pure almond liqueur
125 g/4 oz/½ cup ground almonds

pan from the heat and spoon the fruit butter into hot, sterilised jars. Seal and label the jars and when cool, refrigerate. It will keep for 2 to 3 months in the fridge. For longer storage, process the jars in a boiling water bath, using the method on p.33.

Lavender-scented damson cheese

Damson cheese is a traditional English sweetmeat, made in the same way as the Brazilians use guavas to make *goiabada* and the Spanish quinces for *membrillo*. Serve it with cheese for a perfect marriage; almost any cheese will work, but I particularly like this with farmhouse Lancashire, a semi-fresh goat cheese or a soft blue sheep cheese such as Roquefort.

Damsons have a large pit, and thus will yield only about half their weight in fruit pulp.

Put the damsons in a saucepan with the water, just enough to stop the fruit from sticking before the juices have been released. Cook the fruit until soft. Rub through a sieve, weigh the pulp, and then weigh out an equal quantity of sugar, using all the lavender sugar and as much sugar as you need to make up the same weight as the damson pulp.

Put the damson pulp in a saucepan, and cook to reduce it by a quarter to a third to remove some of the water content. Meanwhile, warm the sugar, and then add it to the fruit pulp. Stir over a low heat until the sugar has dissolved, and then cook until the mixture thickens sufficiently to part when a spoon is drawn through it. Pack into straight-sided pots, loaf tins or flat, round sponge tins, and leave overnight to set. The

**makes about 750 g/
1 ½ lbs/3 cups**

1 kg/2 lbs damsons
125 ml/4 fl oz/½ cup water
125 g/4 oz/½ cup lavender
  sugar
375 g/12 oz/1 ½ cups sugar
  – see recipe

pots can then be covered and sealed. If you set the cheese in a loaf tin or sponge tin, it can be turned out, sliced or cut into wedges and closely wrapped in wax paper and foil for storage.

Cook's tip

This is an excellent preserve that will repay keeping for several months. By then, it will be beginning to shrink away from the sides of its containers and the sugar may start to crystallise on the surface and at the edges. These are signs not of deterioration but that all is well.

Rose-scented quince paste

Time-consuming to make, but well worth it for lovely Christmas presents, quince paste is particularly economical in that it uses the pulp left over after making quince jelly. Sieving the pulp is the hardest part of the recipe.

This is excellent served with a mature hard cheese, with a blue cheese or a soft goat cheese, in fact, with the perfect cheeseboard.

Rub the pulp from jelly-making through a sieve into a pan, stir in the sugar, and cook gently until the sugar has dissolved. Simmer until the mixture is a translucent garnet colour, thick enough to remain separated when you draw a spoon across the bottom of the pan. Remove the pan from the heat. Spoon the mixture into a dish or cake tin, lightly oiled with a neutral oil, such as almond or peanut, and let the mixture set. Cut into wedges to serve or, for longer storage, pack it into steril-ised straight-sided pots and leave overnight to set. The pots can then be covered and sealed. It will keep in the fridge for one or two years.

makes about 500 g/1 lb/2 cups

500 g/1 lb/2 cups quince pulp (p.62)
375 g/12 oz/1 ½ cups granulated sugar
125 g/4 oz/½ cup rose petal sugar (p.26)

Golden rose petal butter

I usually use deep pink or red scented roses for cooking, but this recipe was inspired by a neighbour's rosebush, hanging over the garden wall, with its large flowers and tightly furled petals, so typical of an old-fashioned rose. Its rich golden colour made me think of butter, and this is the result. It is similar in texture to brandy butter, and can be used in the same way.

Put the butter, sugar, and rose petals in a food processor and blend until smooth. Taste, and add the rosewater if you feel it needs a little boost of flavour.

Cook's tip

If you freeze the butter, you will have something unusual to serve with the Christmas pudding. And if you use it fresh, serve it with a peach and almond crumble. Of course, using red or deep pink roses as an alternative in this recipe, will produce a most striking preserve. Try it with crêpes.

makes about 375 g/12 oz/ 1 ½ cups

250 g/8 oz/2 sticks unsalted butter, at room temperature

250 g/8 oz/1 ¼ cups powdered sugar

4 heaped tablespoons scented yellow rose petals, freshly picked and perfectly dry

Rosewater, optional – see recipe

Good things in bottles

"I love bright red drinks, don't you? They taste twice as good as any other colour," says Anne in *Anne of Green Gables*. Some of mine are red, some yellow, some purple, each as good as the other.

Liquid fragrant fruit, enhanced with a hint of flowers, makes wonderfully refreshing drinks in summer, diluted with still or sparkling water, and can be used to make creative cocktails. They are also delicious poured over ice cream. Apricots, blackberries, cherries, dates, grapes, and mulberries are some of the fruit you can use, as well as, of course, lemons and limes, for syrups and cordials.

Because pectin is not required in the making of syrup, you can use very ripe, almost overripe, fruit provided it is not spoilt in any way. The cleaned fruit is cooked in just enough water to allow the juices to run free, then the fruit is mashed, the pulp squeezed, not dripped, through a jelly bag, and 500 g/1 lb/2 cups of sugar added for each 500 ml/17 fl oz/2 cups of juice.

Rose, lavender, clove pink, and jasmine are the flowers which work best with fruit, and also orange flower water.

Flower syrups

Sugar preserves the flavour and colour of sweetly scented flowers, which can be used alone, without any fruit. The amount of sugar you need depends on how you plan to use the syrup. To make a poaching syrup, you will use two parts water to one part sugar. For a medium-weight syrup, of the kind you would use to soak a rum baba for example, equal volumes of water and sugar are required. For a keeping syrup, use one and a half to two parts sugar to one part water.

This last syrup is really the most useful, as you can dilute it to make a poaching syrup. This heavy or strong syrup is ideal for spooning over ice creams, or a steamed pudding in winter, for diluting with mineral water for a refreshing drink, and for using as the sweet element in cocktails.

More flavour can be obtained by repeating the maceration process. That is, once you have soaked the petals overnight, strain the liquid into a saucepan, bring it to the boil, and pour it over a fresh batch of petals before proceeding to make the syrup. Roses, violets, jasmine, and carnations can be prepared this way. For lavender, one maceration is sufficient, and you only need 6 to 8 flower heads for the volume of sugar and water below.

Infusing the more delicate petals in boiling syrup is less successful because the mixture is too dense to penetrate the flowers, especially with a heavy syrup, and there is no release of colour. Whereas boiling water poured over even a small quantity of lavender flowers will release a wonderful clear blue colour, lavender will also flavour a boiling syrup because of the intensity of the essential oils in the flowers. With roses it can be a little disconcerting to see that the water might turn a pale yellow/green as the petals are infusing. But when you add the sugar, the syrup turns a lovely and quite deep natural pink.

Syrups should not be kept for longer than a year as colour and flavour begin to deteriorate after that, even when stored in a cool dark pantry. If you plan to store rather than refrigerate the syrup or cordial for fairly immediate use, syrups and cordials must be sterilised in the bottle, using the boiling water bath method on p.33 to prevent them from fermenting.

Flower syrup

Boil the water, pour it over the flower petals and leave overnight. For extra flavour, do a second maceration and put another 50 g/2 oz/ ¼ cup flower petals in a nonreactive bowl. Bring the first floral liquid back to the boil, pour it over the fresh flower petals, and once again leave overnight. Then put all the ingredients in a saucepan and heat gently until the sugar has dissolved. Bring to the boil, simmer for 2 or 3 minutes before removing from the heat, and let cool until cold. Strain into a sterilised bottle and label.

makes about three 250 ml/ 8 oz bottles

500 ml/17 fl oz/2 cups water
50 g/2 oz/¼ cup single variety
    flower petals, such as
    jasmine, rose, elderflower,
    violet, gorse, carnation,
    myrtle – but see recipe
500 g/1 lb/2 cups granulated
    sugar

Pomegranate and jasmine syrup

As well as in desserts, I use this syrup to marinate and glaze game, poultry, and lamb. At Christmas one year I prepared pheasant breasts marinated in pomegranate syrup and walnut oil, finished off on a charcoal grill. Another year it was sliced pan-fried turkey breasts, marinated in pomegranate syrup and served with a delicate sauce, decorated with pomegranate seeds.

The syrup also makes the most wonderful margaritas.

makes 250 ml/1 cup

12 pomegranates
75 g/3 oz/½ cup jasmine
    flowers

To obtain pomegranate juice, hold the fruit steady and, with a sharp knife, cut a thin slice from the stem end of the fruit, revealing the juicy scarlet seeds close-packed inside. Stand the fruit upright and make five or six knife cuts down through the skin only. Take care not to puncture the seeds as you do this. With your fingers, separate out the four or five sections, then bend each back and push off the seeds. Remove the bitter pith and membranes and discard. To extract the juice, use the back of a spoon to crush the seeds in a plastic sieve placed over a bowl. Or simply halve the fruit and extract the juice by gently but firmly pressing each half over a lemon juicer. It is not a good idea to use an electric or even mechanical means of extracting the juice as this breaks down the seeds and membrane and makes the juice taste too bitter.

Prepare the pomegranates as described above, extracting as much juice as possible. You should have about 1 litre/1 ¾ pint/4 cups. Pour it into a nonreactive saucepan and cook gently until reduced by about a third. Add the jasmine flowers and simmer until reduced by a third, by which time the mixture will be quite thick. Remove the pan from the heat. Strain and decant the syrup into a hot, sterilised bottle, cork, and label.

If you want to make larger quantities for long storage, then you should process the syrup following the water bath method on p.33.

Cook's tip

Unlike some of the other recipes, the syrup is simply the concentrated juice, without the addition of sugar, so it still retains a sharp note of acidity. If you reduce the mixture further, you will have pomegranate molasses.

Rose-scented pomegranate syrup

Grenadine, or pomegranate syrup, is traditional in France and Italy for flavouring long drinks and ices. Pomegranate juice on its own is one of the best marinades I know, with a real depth of distinctive flavour, adding colour to the final sauce as might a light red wine. Best of all, it has just the right balance of acidity.

Flavouring it with a hint of roses, I use this syrup to glaze poultry and light meat game birds, as well as lamb. And it makes the most exquisite drink when mixed with champagne, cava, or other sparkling wine.

To juice the pomegranates, follow the method described in the previous recipe.

You should have about 1 litre/1 ¾ pint/4 cups of juice. Pour it into a nonreactive saucepan and cook gently with the rose petals until reduced by half. Remove the pan from the heat, strain the juice into another saucepan to which you stir in the rosewater and sugar. Bring to the boil, simmer for 3 or 4 minutes, and remove from the heat. Decant the syrup into hot, sterilised bottles, cork, and label.

If you want to make large quantities for long storage, then you should process the syrup following the water bath method on p.33.

makes about three 250 ml/ 8 oz bottles

12 pomegranates
3 tablespoons dried rose petals
2 teaspoons rosewater
500 g/1 lb/2 cups granulated sugar – see recipe

Jasmine tea syrup

Easy to make, just one stage on from brewing a pot of tea, this is a most versatile bottle. Refreshing summer drinks, flavouring for a mayonnaise to accompany cured salmon, a glaze for grilled chicken breasts, jasmine tea syrup also has its place in cocktails.

Put the tea and extra jasmine flowers in a teapot. Boil the water and brew the tea in the usual way, leaving it for about 5 minutes. Strain it into a saucepan and add the sugar. Bring to the boil, simmer for a couple of minutes, then remove from the heat, pour into sterilised bottles, seal, and label. Store in a cool dark place for 3 to 4 months; for longer storage, process in a water bath – see p.33.

makes three 250 ml/8 oz bottles

2 to 3 teaspoons jasmine tea
1 tablespoon fresh jasmine flowers
500 ml/17 fl oz/2 cups water
500 ml/1 lb/2 cups granulated sugar

Elderflower cordial

Elderflower cordial or syrup makes a wonderfully refreshing drink, diluted with sparkling mineral water. A half shot mixed with gin and lemon zest makes a lovely summery martini. I also use it to flavour custards, sorbets and ice creams; it is especially good with strawberries. It is worth making several bottles every year, to last until the next season.

Put the sugar and water in a saucepan, dissolve the sugar and bring it to the boil. Remove the lemon zest in thin slivers and squeeze the juice. Drop the flower heads into the syrup, together with the lemon zest and juice. Bring back to the boil. Stir in the citric acid, remove the pan from the heat, and cover the pan with a doubled paper towel. Leave

makes about 1 litre/ 1 ¾ pint/1 US quart

1.5 kg/3 lb/5 cups granulated sugar
1 litre/1 ¾ pint/4 cups water
15 elderflower heads, well shaken, stalks removed
Zest and juice of 2 lemons
1 to 2 teaspoons citric acid

for 24 hours before straining into sterilised bottles. Keeps for 2 to 3 months, or longer if refrigerated.

Cook's tip

Add the smaller amount of citric acid first, and use more only if you think it needs it. To me, too much will give the flavour of a highly processed commercial product.

Fennel flower, lemon, and scented herb cordial

I make this in my Gozo kitchen in January, with the new season's lemons and wild fennel which I gather in the countryside. Which other herbs you use will depend on what you can find or buy.

Thinly pare off the lemon zest and put it in a saucepan together with the fennel and geranium leaves. Pour on 750 ml/1 ¼ pint/3 cups of boiling water. Simmer for 10 minutes then remove from the heat and leave to infuse until cold. Halve and squeeze the lemons and add the juice to the pan, together with the sugar. Bring to the boil, making sure all the sugar has dissolved, simmer for a minute, then remove from the heat. When cool, strain into sterilised bottles. Keep in the fridge for immediate use. Or process as in the method on p.33 and, once cooled and labelled, store in the pantry.

makes three 250 ml/8 oz bottles

4 unwaxed lemons
8 fennel flower heads
6 scented geranium, lemon verbena or linden blossom leaves
Small sprig of lemon thyme
500 g/1 lb/2 cups granulated sugar

Cook's tip

The lemon zest will have absorbed some of the syrup and retained some flavour, so I keep it for using in a cake or ice cream, snipping it into shreds with sharp scissors and storing it in an airtight container in the fridge or freezer until I need it.

Bitter lemon cordial, with a hint of lavender

This is far better than any bottled bitter lemon drink you might buy, and a very good thing to have to hand, whatever the season. Dilute a tablespoon or so in a glass of chilled sparkling water for a most refreshing drink. For a sundowner, add a measure of gin and a dash of bitters.

Put all the ingredients in a saucepan over low heat. Let the sugar dissolve, then bring to the boil, remove from the heat and steep overnight. The bitterness comes from the number of seeds you let escape into the juice. More than 6 or 8 and you might find it too bitter; leave out seeds altogether and the cordial will not be bitter. Strain into sterilised bottles and keep in the fridge, or process in a water bath (see p.33) and store in the pantry once cooled and labelled.

makes three or four 250 ml/
8 oz bottles

500 ml/17 fl oz/2 cups water
Thinly peeled zest and juice
  of 6-8 lemons, including
  seeds 500 g/1 lb/2 cups
  granulated sugar
½ teaspoon dried lavender
  flowers

Carnation wine cordial

Sops-in-wine is a variety of small clove pink, named after the drink served to couples on their betrothal in medieval England, the flower petals floating in the wine. My spiced and fragrant version evokes something like a vermouth. Enjoy it as a long drink with a slice of orange and sparkling mineral water, splash it on a summer salad of strawberries and raspberries or, use it in a sauce to accompany summer pudding.

Put the water and flower petals in a saucepan. Bring to the boil and leave to steep overnight. Strain into a saucepan, add the sugar, spices and orange zest, bring to the boil, simmer for 5 minutes, remove from the heat, and leave

makes four 250 ml/8 oz
bottles

250 ml/8 fl oz/1 cup water
75 g/3 oz/½ cup clove pink
  or carnation flowers
250 g/8 oz/1 cup granulated
  sugar
6 cloves
Seeds of 2 cardamom pods
Generous curl of thinly pared
  orange zest
One 750 ml bottle full-bodied
  red wine
2 tablespoons brandy

overnight. Strain the liquid into a large jug, stir in the wine and brandy, then pour into sterilised bottles, seal, and label. Unopened, this will keep for a few months in the pantry. Once opened, keep it in the fridge and use within 4 to 6 weeks.

Vino aromatizado con naranja

This was a wine much enjoyed by Jerezano families in the past, and some still make it today. I have also come across something similar in Liguria, where olive leaves and orange zest were used to flavour brandy, which produces something like a home-made *amaro* or bitter. A splash poured into a still-hot but empty espresso cup makes a perfect ending to a meal.

Peel off long, thin strips of orange zest, put them in a decanter, and fill it with cream sherry. Rub the sugar cube over the orange to take up the rest of the fragrant essential oils, add it to the decanter, together with a splash of Iberian brandy and orange flower water. Leave this *vino aromatizado* for several weeks and then serve it in small glasses as a *digestivo*.

Cook's tip

As well as a digestive, I also find this very good indeed for cooking – just a dash used in a duck casserole makes all the difference.

makes one 750 ml bottle

2 bitter oranges
1 bottle cream sherry
1 sugar cube
1 to 2 tablespoons Spanish brandy
1 to 2 tablespoons orange flower water

Ratafias, liqueurs and flavoured spirits

Unlike syrups and cordials, these preserves are spirit-based, some with sugar, some perfectly dry. Some of them are made by macerating the ingredients in the spirit, in order to draw out the flavour compounds. The liqueur is then bottled to produce a fragrant ratafia. You can also crush the fruit, strain off the juices, mix with floral sugar or fresh flowers and then spirit, to make a fruit liqueur. All of these are useful in cocktails, as well as to splash on ice creams or sorbets.

Spirits are perfect for extracting the flavour and colour from flowers. Elderflowers, roses, carnations, jasmine macerated in gin, vodka, or grappa give excellent results, and you do not need to buy premium spirits; a neutral, unflavoured one is best. Lavender is a little more difficult to handle. Using lavender and spirits alone produces something akin to *eau de lavande,* which one wants to avoid at all costs. And unfortunately, at one stage, if you are using vibrantly coloured fresh lavender, purple-hued meth-ylated spirit comes to mind. But with judicious combina-tions of fruit and or herbs, some exciting cocktails can be devised.

Myrtle ratafia

Bruise the spices, flowers, and leaves in a mortar, put them in a wide-necked jar or decanter, and pour in the brandy. Close and leave to infuse for 5 days. Make a syrup with the sugar and about 3 tablespoons water, heating gently until the sugar has dissolved. Mix with the infused brandy, strain through fine muslin or a sieve, then bottle and label.

**makes about 1 litre/
1 ¾ pint/1 US quart**

1 nutmeg, sliced
6 cloves
6 tablespoons myrtle flowers
8 myrtle leaves
2 bay leaves
1 750 ml bottle of brandy
250 g/8 oz/1 cup sugar

Lavender *cassis*

Make your own scented version of the French blackcurrant liqueur and you will always have on hand the key ingredient of a Kir, a simple and delicious aperitif. Pour the *cassis* over raspberry sorbet for a truly fabulous taste sensation.

Put the blackcurrants and water in a saucepan and cook until the fruit is just soft. Strain the fruit through a muslin-lined sieve or jelly bag suspended over a saucepan. Stir in the sugar, add the lavender, bring this to the boil, and remove from the heat. Allow the syrup to cool completely, then stir in the vodka, decant into bottles, cork, and label.

**makes about 1.5 litres/
2 ½ pints/1 ½ US quarts**

1 kg/2 lb blackcurrants
250 ml/8 fl oz/1 cup water
500 g/2 cups granulated
  sugar
½ teaspoon lavender flowers
  tied in muslin
1 750 ml bottle vodka

Very cherry – and rose

An extraordinarily good year for cherries was the inspiration for this ratafia. Not only was I able to find luscious English cherries in the local farmers' market and inexpensive stalkless cherries from Jerte in Spain, but also wild cherries from trees on Hampstead Heath. I have never before been able to get to them before the birds. This particular year there was enough for all of us.

I deliberated whether to add sugar to make a cherry liqueur, but in the end we liked the dry, yet full fruit flavour so much that I bottled it without sugar. You can drink this lovely red drink at room temperature or keep a bottle in the freezer. Either way works for an excellent *digestif*. Splash it on a fruit salad, flavour a custard for cherry clafoutis, deglaze a pan of chicken livers…. Endless possibilities.

**makes three 250 ml/8 fl oz
bottles**

500 g/1 lb cherries
3 handfuls very scented fresh
  red rose petals
1 bottle gin

All that is required is a little patience to slit the cherries and drop them into a jug along with the rose petals. Wild cherries can be squeezed lightly and the pit pops out. This you can discard. Pour the gin over the fruit and petals and seal the top with cling film. Leave it for as long as you can, at least 3 weeks, but you might have to keep tasting it to see how it is developing. Too many tastes, and you will probably want to add more cherries and more gin.

Once sufficiently infused, strain the gin, bottle it, and label. The colour will begin to fade after 6 months or so, but the flavour will still be there. If the cherries are too good to discard, use them in a clafoutis, or follow the recipe for sloe gin jelly on p.67.

Fragrant *limoncello*

Excellent in cooking, or splashed on ice cream, this also makes a heavenly martini. And I keep a bottle in the freezer to serve when a *digestif* is called for.

Carefully peel the zest from the lemons without removing any white pith, which would make the liqueur bitter. Put the zest and lavender in a glass jug or decanter, of at least 1 litre/1 ¾ pint/1 US quart capacity, ensuring that the lavender bundle is suspended and accessible, and fill to the top with vodka. Cover the top with cling film and keep, ideally on a sunny window sill, for 3 or 4 weeks, but do a taste test after a couple of days to check that the lavender flavour is right for you. You might want to remove the flowers at that point, or leave them a little longer.

makes about 2 litres/3 ½ pints/2 US quarts

8 unwaxed lemons

½ teaspoon lavender flowers tied in muslin, with a long piece of kitchen string – see recipe

1 litre/1 ¾ pint/1 US quart bottle vodka

1 kg/2 lbs/4 cups sugar

Once you have sealed the container of vodka and zest, halve and squeeze the lemons and make up the juice to 1 litre/1 ¾ pint/4 cups with water. Put it in a nonreactive saucepan with the sugar and simmer until the sugar has dissolved. Bring to the boil, remove from the heat and store the lemon syrup until the lemon zest has infused the vodka sufficiently.

Strain the syrup into a large jug, then strain in the flavoured vodka. Mix well then pour the pale yellow liquid, which will be cloudy, not clear, through a funnel into sterilised bottles. Seal with a cork or screw top, and label.

Cook's tip

I use the vodka-soaked lemon zest in baking. First I let the zest dry out then I grind it with sugar and use that as some or all of the sugar required in cake recipes.

Sloe and damson gin with a hint of rose

The hedgerow where I forage has both sloe and damson bushes, so I mix the two fruits, but you can use the recipe for either fruit or both. This is traditionally made in the autumn, when the fruit is in season for a short time. Depending on the weather, I find I sometimes have to pick the fruit in August otherwise the birds have taken them. By Christmas, the gin will have developed a rich fruit and almond-like flavour, with the merest breath of roses, and beautiful deep, almost amethyst colour. Use the liqueur in cocktails, or serve small glasses as an after-dinner cordial.

I cannot bear to throw away the soaked fruit once I bottle the gin, so on p.67 you will find a recipe for sloe and damson gin jelly.

makes about 1 litre/1 ¾ pint/1 US quart

500 g/1 lb damsons and/or sloes

1 750 ml bottle gin

375 g/12 oz/1 ½ cups granulated sugar

125 g/4 oz/½ cup rose petal sugar (p.26)

Rinse the fruit and discard any that are damaged, as well as loose leaves and stalks. Prick each fruit all over and put into a large glass jug, wide-necked decanter, or other nonreactive container. Pour on the gin, stir in the sugar, cover, and store for 2 to 3 months, away from the light. For the first few days, shake or stir the mixture to ensure that the sugar dissolves.

Strain the liqueur through fine muslin, bottle it, cork and label, and keep in a dark place. This is even better when kept for up to a year before straining; the fruit flavours are even more concentrated.

Hedgerow gin

This really is one for the foragers. And like the hedgerow jelly, it is a mystery as to what colour and flavour you will achieve in the end; it all depends on your foraging harvest.

This is not unlike a *very* rustic *Rumtopf,* see p.154, in that flowers and fruit are added as the seasons progress. So rather than a recipe, here are some ideas to get started.

Flowers start the process, with elderflowers being the first, which you put in a large glass jug or preserving jar with a bottle of gin poured over them. Even better is an old-fashioned glass sweet jar if you can find one. Then you can add gorse flowers, hawthorn flowers, and apple blossom. By the time wild roses are in bloom, you can add these and the first of the hedgerow fruits – wild cherries if you are lucky. Then as the season progresses, sloes, damsons, blackberries, hips, haws, and elderberries. Add more gin if necessary to keep the fruit and flowers covered. A few crab apples, cut in half, can also be added.

By Christmas, the gin will be ready to strain, bottle, and label.

If you wish, you can make a sweeter, less alcoholic drink by adding one-third volume of sugar syrup and two-thirds gin.

Quince and rose petal ratafia

Preserve the intense scent and flavour of quinces by extracting it into a spirit and combine it with a hint of roses. Like apples and pears, the quince is of the Rosaceae family, which makes its pairing with scented roses both harmonious and logical.

makes about two 250 ml/ 8 oz bottles

2 quinces
2 tablespoons rose petals
500 ml/17 fl oz/1 pint vodka, gin, or grappa

Use the ratafia in cocktails, as an after-dinner drink, poured over a quince or apple sorbet or to *flamber* a hot fruit salad.

Rinse and wipe the quinces thoroughly to remove the down on the skin. Cut the fruit into chunks and pack them into a wide-necked decanter or a preserving jar with the rose petals. Cover the fruit completely with the spirit. Cover the jar or decanter with a piece of cling film and leave to macerate for at least a month, preferably two, before decanting into sterilised bottles, sealing, and labelling.

Lavender, lovage, and tomato vodka

I add the savoury flavours to avoid the *eau de lavande* effect. And nothing is more savoury than tomato water combined with the yeasty flavour of lovage. Use celery leaves if you cannot get lovage. This makes an extraordinary Bloody Mary, replacing your usual vodka.

Roughly chop the tomatoes and place them in muslin-lined sieve to let the clear liquid drip through into a 1 litre/1 ¾ pint/1 US quart jug. This is the liquid found encasing the seeds, and not the red juice from the pulp. You will probably get about 125 ml/4 fl oz/½ cup of tomato water. If you are lucky enough to get more, then use it for something else, such as poaching scallops in it. The chopped pulp you can use for soup, or for the chutney recipe on p.119.

Bruise the lovage leaves in a mortar and put them in the jug with the tomato water. Add the lavender and half the vodka. Cover tightly with cling film and leave to steep for a day, ideally on a sunny windowsill. Strain through muslin into sterilised bottles and top up with vodka. Seal tightly. Turn the bottle upside-down a couple of times, then store in a cool, dark place until required. You will have a little vodka left. I am sure you will find a use for it.

makes three 250 ml/8 oz bottles

1 kg/2 lbs tomatoes
6 sprigs of lovage
3 or 4 fresh lavender heads
1 bottle vodka

Fig and fennel flower vodka

This is a recipe for those lucky enough to have access not only to fresh figs, but also the fig tree, in order to pick the leaves. The newer, tender leaves have more of that elusive 'green' fragrance which I love in fig-based perfumes. If fig leaves are not available, add two or three more fennel flowers.

This would, of course, qualify for a floral recipe without the addition of fennel flowers, since it is the fruit itself which contains the myriad fig flowers.

Quarter the figs and put them in a Kilner jar or similar clip-top jar with the torn-up fig leaves and a scattering of fennel flowers. Fill with vodka. Seal and keep for a couple of weeks at least. Strain the vodka through muslin into a jug, then pour it into sterilised bottles. Seal and label.

makes three 250 ml/8 oz bottles

8 fresh ripe figs, purple or green, depending on season
2 tender fig leaves – see recipe
8 to 10 fennel flower heads
1 bottle vodka

Cook's tip

I use the well-soaked fruit in a crumble with an almond topping.

Bartender's tip

The vodka is perfect with fizzy water and no other addition, but you might also like it with a dash of anise spirit or liqueur.

Elderflower, cucumber, and lemon gin

This has all the flavours of a late English spring and makes a genteel drink for the garden, with the spritz of fizzy water, or cava. It turns a pale lemon green.

With a swivel-blade peeler, remove the cucumber skin in a thin layer and put it in a 2 litre/3 ½ pint/2 US quart jug. Halve the cucumber lengthways, scoop out the seeds, and add these to the pitcher. Roughly chop one half of the cucumber and put in the jug. (Use the rest of the cucumber in a salad.) Take off a thin layer of lemon zest and put it with the cucumber, adding the elderflowers. Pour in half the gin, cover the jug and let it steep for at least 3 days and up to a week, ideally on a sunny window sill.

Strain the mixture through a muslin-lined sieve into a clean jug, and from there decant it into sterilised bottles. Top up the infused gin with the remaining plain gin, until the bottles are full. Seal and label.

makes three 250 ml/8 oz bottles

1 cucumber
Zest of 2 lemons
12 or more elderflower heads
1 bottle London Dry gin

Gorgeous gillyflower grappa

Gillyflower is an old English name for tradi-tional scented pinks and carnations, not modern hybrids. This alliterative drink can be served as a *digestif* or as an ingredient in cocktails.

Roughly crush the cloves in a mortar and put them in a large jug. Add the flower petals and pour on half the grappa. Cover the jug and let the ingredients steep for up to a week, ideally on a sunny window sill.

makes three 250 ml/8 oz bottles

4 cloves
4 heaping tablespoons clove carnation petals
1 bottle grappa

Strain the mixture through a muslin-lined sieve into a clean jug and from there decant it into sterilised bottles. Top up the infused grappa with the remaining plain grappa, until the bottles are full. Seal and label.

Bartender's tip

Flower garden grappa, using a combination of jasmine flowers, rose petals, myrtle blossom, hawthorn blossom, apple blossom, and pinks can be made in the same way. This keeps it light and floral. Add a couple of lavender flowers if you want more punch.

Nocino

On San Giovanni, the feast of St. John, and also Midsummer Day, is when walnuts are picked, while still green and soft-shelled, to make this traditional liqueur in Emilia-Romagna.

Just as fennel flowers work well with the pickled walnuts on p.136, so they do in this Italian walnut liqueur. The anise flavour tends to have a soothing effect on the digestion; rather like the Basque *Patxaran*, which is essentially sloe gin with the addition of star anise.

makes 1 litre/1 ¾ pint/1 US quart

25 whole green walnuts
1 litre/1 ¾ pint/1 US quart alcohol – see below
7.5 cm/3 inch cinnamon stick
4 cloves
1 walnut leaf
1 teaspoon fennel seeds
4 sprigs fennel flowers
500 g/1 lb/2 cups granulated sugar

We first sampled home-made *nocino* at the Lancellotti family's former restaurant near Modena, where they also made *aceto balsamico tradizionale di Modena*, as well as Lambrusco and various traditional grape preserves. This liqueur is suave, dark and powerful, to be sipped in minute quantities.

Cut each walnut lengthways into 6 wedges, and put them in a large glass preserving jar with the alcohol (use two or more smaller containers if necessary) with the spices, walnut leaf and fennel seeds and flowers. Seal the jar and leave it in a warm, sunny place for 2 months, shaking it from time to time. At the end of this period, strain the liquid through a muslin-lined sieve into a large jug or bowl.

In a saucepan, make a syrup with 1 cup of the sugar and 2 tablespoons water and in another, larger saucepan, caramelise the remaining 1 cup sugar. When just brown, but not burnt, remove the pan from the heat and carefully pour in the boiling syrup, stirring all the time. Allow the mixture to cool, then mix the caramel syrup with the walnut extract. Pour into sterilised jars again, seal, and leave for 30 to 40 days, shaking it occasionally. Finally, filter the liqueur into sterilised bottles, seal, and label.

Traditionally, *nocino* is aged for a year, preferably two, before drinking, but you will find that it is quite drinkable by Christmas.

Cook's tip

The bottling alcohol I use is the kind found in French grocers and supermarkets, labelled *eau de vie de fruits*. If unavailable, I suggest grappa or vodka.

In a pickle

Chutney

"All Chatneys should be quite thick, almost of the consistence of mashed turnip or stewed tomatoes, or stiff bread sauce. They are served with curries; and also with steaks, cutlets, cold meat and fish."Eliza Acton, *Modern Cookery for Private Families,* 1845

Quite. Miss Acton has it exactly right. It would be a mistake to think of chutneys as only suitable to accompany curries. These are amongst my favourite preserves, with deep, rich flavours and strong, hot notes of chilli and vinegar, enhanced with flowers such as lavender or fennel. Preserved with vinegar, salt, and sugar the process involved in making chutneys is simply long slow cooking. The mixture does not jell but thickens as the water evaporates from the fruit and vegetables used. A heat-diffusing mat is useful to maintain a low simmer without burning the contents of the pan. When making chutneys, pickles, and any other preserve which requires vinegar to be cooked, it is best to choose a day when you can open the kitchen windows – the smell of cooking vinegar is very pervasive.

All chutneys are best kept for at least two months before using, although they taste good within a few days of making them.

Traditionally, they were made in the autumn and opened at Christmas, the perfect accompaniment to holiday buffets and platters of cold cuts.

Pickles

"Only a pickled peach can beat a good pickled walnut, and not always then." Henry Sarson, *Home Pickling* (1940). This was the book for all those who had forgotten or "never knew how to make pickles like mother used to make," for enthusiastic allotment growers whose surpluses rotted in the tool shed and for greenhouse owners whose last tomatoes failed to ripen in "the fickle English sun."

One of the differences between a chutney and a pickle is that generally chutney is made with sugar, and pickles are made without. However, I like to use sugar in some of my pickles, so I do not know if this makes them chuckles or pickneys. Also, pickles are made from raw or lightly cooked vegetables, and are therefore crisp. Floral flavours combine nicely with many pickles, in the same way that herbs and spices do, but I'm not sure that Henry Sarson would have approved.

Ketchup

A finely balanced combination of fruit, or vegetable, with sugar, vinegar and spices, together with a floral hint, ketchups are an excellent addition to the array of home-made preserves. Kiwi fruit and elderflower or mango and jasmine ketchup can be used in just the same way as one might use tomato ketchup, but are infinitely more exotic. You can make them for immediate use, and for storing in the refrigerator for a few weeks, but in order to keep ketchup for a few months, it must be processed in a boiling water bath (p.33). The reason is that unlike chutneys and pickles, the concentration of sugar and vinegar is too low to preserve it. And one cannot increase the quantities without overpowering the flavour of the fruit or vegetable, the scent of the jasmine or elderflower.

Salsas

Most salsa recipes are a mixture of low-acid vegetables and
fruit, such as onions, chillies, peppers, mango, and pineapple
combined with more acidic ingredients such as tomatoes. Sugar
may or may not be used. In classic salsas, herbs and spices are
often added for extra flavour, and I like to add flowers to mine.
They will keep in the refrigerator for a few weeks, but if you
are using up a glut of tomatoes or other ingredients, you will
be making larger quantities and will want to store the salsa for
longer. This will require it to be processed in a boiling water
bath (p.33)

Use only high-quality tomatoes, mangoes, and other fruit at
their peak, neither under- nor overripe. Acid should be added
when making a salsa for storing because the natural acidity in the
fruit may not be high enough.

Spices, herbs, and flowers add flavour to ketchups and salsas.
Coriander, peppercorns, cloves, chillies, and cumin are the
spices most often used, and I like to use fresh mint, fennel or
fennel flowers, elderflowers, clove pinks, lavender, and jasmine,
depending on the fruit I am using.

Floral vinegars

Flavoured vinegars have been part of the cook's repertoire for
hundreds of years, especially for the country cook, who had
access to a wealth of wildflowers. Flower vinegars are excellent
as a dressing for delicate salad leaves, and also warm salads of fish
or chicken. You can also use them in mayonnaise and hollandaise
sauce. If you are making fruit chutneys, consider using a flower
vinegar, perhaps rose vinegar for a fig chutney, elderflower
vinegar in gooseberry chutney, and lavender vinegar in an apple.
Sweet cucumber pickles are very good done in an elderflower
vinegar, as are pickled herrings or salmon.

I generally use white wine vinegar as I like to see the contents
of the bottle, but elderflowers are very good in cider vinegar,
and there is no reason not to use red wine vinegar if you wish

to make to make a fragrant red rose vinegar. However, there are many excellent vinegars, not all made from wine, but rice vinegar and coconut vinegar, for example, which can be flavoured with jasmine. Moscatel wine vinegar from Spain is the perfect vehicle for more delicate flower vinegars, especially elderflower, carnation and, rose. Flowers from myrtle, sage, and fennel can also be used.

When I am in Gozo in late spring, one of my kitchen tasks is to refresh my *acetaia*. Nothing like the small varied wooden barrels my Modenese friends keep in their attic, full of the precious essence of *aceto balsamico tradizionale di Modena*, my vinegars are in a collection of the more decorative white wine bottles, sterilised and filled with white wine vinegar, variously flavoured with fennel flowers, rose petals, lavender, sage flowers, and elderflowers.

I take each bottle and pour the contents into a pitcher through muslin. I rinse out the bottle with scalding water and dry them in the oven for 15 to 20 minutes at 112°C/250°F, which also sterilises them. I then put fresh flowers in the bottle, three or four sprigs of lavender, for example, rather more for rose petal vinegar, perhaps 2 tablespoons. I pour in the strained vinegar and top up the space with fresh white wine vinegar. Thus the vinegar goes through something like the Spanish *solera* system, the old vinegar 'educating' the new vinegar, and fresh ingredients adding their flavour. The vinegar I use there is a fairly standard, widely available, Italian white wine vinegar; choosing white simply to allow the herbs or flowers to show through. Naturally, the vinegar does darken over the course of the year, although at the beginning of the season it is clear and elegant.

Tomato and lavender chutney

As in other recipes, lavender combines perfectly with tomatoes and adds a subtle flavour to this simple chutney.

Peel and seed the tomatoes, and dice them. Quarter, peel, and core the apples and dice them – or briefly chop in the food processor. Peel the onion and trim the celery. Finely chop both.

Put all the ingredients in a nonreactive saucepan and cook on a low heat for 45 to 60 minutes, stirring from time to time, and more frequently toward the end of cooking as the liquid evaporates and the mixture becomes more jammy.

Remove the lavender bundle. Spoon the hot chutney into hot sterilised jars. Seal the jars, label, and store in a cool, dry place. This chutney will keep for 2 to 3 months, no longer because it does not contain a lot of vinegar and sugar. For longer storage, process in a water bath – see p.33.

makes four 400 g/14 oz jars

1 kg/2 lbs tomatoes
500 g/1 lb tart apples
2 onions
1 celery stalk
250 ml/8 fl oz/1 cup wine
   vinegar, red or white
250 g/8 oz/1 cup light
   muscovado or other soft
   light brown sugar
1 teaspoon lavender flowers,
   tied in muslin
2 cloves
2 star anise pods
2 teaspoons grated fresh
   ginger
1 teaspoon salt

Tomato and wild garlic flower chutney

Just a faint hint of garlic from the delicate wild flowers flavours this simple chutney which I make in spring, before tomatoes are ripe and plentiful, but the hedgerows are full of wild garlic.

Put all the ingredients in a large, nonreactive saucepan and bring to the boil. Simmer for about an hour until the mixture thickens to a pulpy consistency, stirring from time to time

makes about three 250 g/ 8 oz jars

2 x 400 g/14 oz cans
   chopped tomatoes in juice
1 large mild white onion,
   peeled and diced
12 to 15 wild garlic flowers on
   stalks, the stalks chopped
   like chives

to prevent sticking. Remove the pan from the heat and allow the mixture to cool a little. Stir and then spoon into hot, sterilised jars, seal and label.

Sicilian carrot chutney

This is much milder than a traditional English chutney, indeed, it is referred to as a *patè*, as it contains little vinegar, so it needs processing in order to preserve it. Alternatively, you can store it in an airtight container in the fridge for use within a week or so. The carrots should, of course, be the sweetest you can find, and carry on the sweetness with a medium to sweet Marsala. It is a versatile recipe, and can be made smooth or chunky as you prefer. Smooth, it makes a perfect topping for *bruschetta*, underneath a curl of *prosciutto* or some crisped *pancetta,* an anchovy fillet, or a couple of black olives.

Cook the carrots in the water and vinegar for about 20 minutes. Drain them and put in a food processor with the rest of the ingredients. Process to the texture you prefer and spoon into small jars. Gently pour on 2 teaspoons of olive oil and close the jars with the appropriate lids. Keep in the fridge.

If storing the chutney at ambient temperature, process the jars in a water bath as described on p.33 for 30 minutes.

1 fresh red chilli, halved, seeds discarded and thinly sliced
6 cardamom pods, cracked
250 g/8 oz/1 cup sugar
250 ml/8 fl oz/1 cup vinegar
1 teaspoon salt

makes four 200 g/7 oz jars

6 to 8 large carrots, peeled and sliced
1 litre/1 ¾ pint/4 cups water
150 ml/5 fl oz white wine vinegar
100 ml/4 fl oz extra-virgin olive oil – plus extra
1 shallot, peeled
4 cloves garlic, peeled
3 tablespoons Marsala – see recipe
2 tablespoons orange flower water
½ teaspoon black pepper

Peach and rose petal chutney

Peach and rose chutney makes a good accompaniment to cold meats, smoked fish and, because it is mild rather than chilli hot, is an excellent condiment to serve with fresh goat cheese.

Put the sugar and vinegar in a nonreactive saucepan and bring to the boil. Add the rest of the ingredients, bring to the boil, reduce the heat, and simmer until you have a thick, spooning consistency. Remove the pan from the heat.

Pot the chutney in hot, sterilised jars and seal and label.

makes about four 250 g/ 8 oz jars

500 g/1 lb/2 cups granulated sugar
500 ml/17 fl oz/2 cups cider vinegar
1 tart apple, peeled, cored and chopped
8 peaches, stones discarded, and each cut into 8 pieces
1 onion, chopped
1 teaspoon ground cloves
1 teaspoon ground cinnamon
1 teaspoon ground allspice
1 teaspoon ground cardamom
3 heaping tablespoons rose petals
2 teaspoons salt

Sweet fennel and onion chutney

This is delicious served as part of a mezze or hors d'oeuvres, with, for example, sardines, hard boiled eggs, and olives.

Gently fry the onion in the oil for 10 to 15 minutes, and then add the fennel, wine, fennel seeds, and ginger. Continue cooking for 15 to 20 minutes, stirring from time to time to prevent sticking. Add the salt and pepper, and stir in the dried fruit, nuts, and wine vinegar. Bring to the boil and boil briskly for 5 minutes, ensuring that the vegetables are quite soft before adding the sugar. Then cook until the mixture has a soft consistency and the vinegar and cooking

makes about four 250 g/ 8 oz jars

4 large mild onions, thinly sliced
6 tablespoons extra-virgin olive oil
3 large fennel bulbs, sliced
6 tablespoons dry white wine
½ teaspoon fennel seeds
1 teaspoon freshly grated ginger
1 teaspoon salt
1 teaspoon freshly ground black pepper
3 tablespoons sultanas or raisins

juices have been absorbed. Strip the flowers from the fennel heads and stir these in at the last minute. Remove the pan from the heat and pot the chutney in hot, sterilised jars. Heat process if you wish, see p.33, then seal and label the jars.

3 tablespoons toasted pine
  nuts or flaked almonds
250 ml/8 fl oz/1 cup white
  wine vinegar
250 g/8 oz/1 cup sugar
4 or 5 fennel flower heads

Plum and raspberry lavender chutney

Cold roast beef or pork sandwiches are delicious with this mellow, spiced chutney.

Put the sugar and vinegar in a nonreactive saucepan and bring to the boil, add the rest of the ingredients, bring back to the boil, reduce the heat, and simmer until the chutney thickens. Remove the pan from the heat. Pot the chutney in hot, sterilised jars, seal and label.

**makes about six 250 g/
8 oz jars**

500 g/1 lb/2 cups sugar
500 ml/17 fl oz/2 cups
  raspberry lavender vinegar
  (p.137)
1 large mild onion, chopped
2 tart apples, peeled, cored,
  and chopped
1.5 kg/3 lbs plums, quartered
  with the stones discarded
½ teaspoon ground cloves
½ teaspoon ground cinnamon

Gooseberry and elderflower chutney

I like to serve this mellow chutney with a 'tasty Lancashire,' but it does well with all traditional farmhouse cheeses.

Cook the gooseberries, apple, and onion to a pulp in just enough water to prevent from burning. Add the vinegar and spices, stir in the sugar and, when it has dissolved, cook the mixture until thick. Remove from the heat and pot in hot sterilised jars. Seal and label them.

makes about eight 250 g/8 oz jars

2 kg/4 lbs gooseberries, topped and tailed
1 large Granny Smith or other tart apple, peeled, cored, and sliced
1 large mild onion, chopped
Water – see recipe
500 ml/17 fl oz/2 cups elderflower vinegar (p.136)
1 teaspoon black peppercorns
Seeds of 6 cardamom pods
1 kg/2 lbs/4 cups sugar

La salsa di estate da Mama Ida

This pickle is based on a recipe I learned in the kitchen of our friends, the Lancellottis, in a village near Modena as we prepared family Sunday lunch. Fresh ingredients from their organic vegetable garden were preserved for later in the year, in this bright, refreshing summer pickle. Their garden was also full of edible flowers of which they made good use in delicate and colourful salads. I have added some to the pickle; the choice of vegetables is less important than their freshness.

Prepare the first four vegetables, peeling and topping and tailing as appropriate, and finely dice. Peel the peppers with a swivel-blade potato peeler, quarter and discard the seeds, then cut into strips. Cook the hard vegetables for 8 minutes with salt, sugar, oil, and vinegar,

makes about 3 kg/6 lbs/3 US quarts

2 onions
4 carrots
6 to 8 celery stalks
500 g/1 lb green beans
6 large red peppers
1 tablespoon salt
1 tablespoon sugar
250 ml/8 fl oz/1 cup extra virgin olive oil
1.5 litres/2 ½ pints/6 cups white wine vinegar
1 tablespoon fennel flowers

and then add the peppers and the flowers.
Cook for 7 minutes, 15 minutes in all.

When cooked, set aside to cool, spoon into jars
with the liquid, and cover with 2.5 cm/
1 inch of olive oil. Seal and label. This will
keep for a year. The Lancellottis would
serve this refreshing pickle with *bollito misto*,
garnished with chopped hard-boiled eggs.

Another summer pickle

This recipe is based on one from my *Times
Cookbook* (1993), which means it must have
been in one of my columns, where I would
have written about what inspired the unusual
combination of ingredients. Because this
is a preparation designed for more or less
immediate use, I have given the number of
servings rather than yield in jars.

It is a colourful, piquant, sweet and sour
pickle, to be served with drinks, just as you
would olives.

Blanch the onions in boiling water for 2 to 3
minutes, then drain and put in a large glass bowl
with the rest of the vegetables and fruit and the
lavender. Put the salt, sugar, cumin, coriander,
olive oil, and vinegar in a small saucepan and
bring to the boil. Remove the pan from the
heat, and stir in the Kirsch, if using it. Pour the
liquid over the vegetables, mix well and seal,
with cling film. Leave for 3 to 4 days before
serving.

Cook's tip

As a fresh pickle, it will not keep for more than a week or
so in the fridge. If you want to keep it longer, which is well

serves 12 to 18 – see recipe

12 small onions, peeled
12 black olives
12 green olives
12 very fresh button
    mushrooms, wiped
12 radishes, topped and tailed
12 cherries
12 yellow cherry or miniature
    plum tomatoes
2 heads new season's garlic,
    cloves separated and peeled
1 teaspoon lavender, tied in
    muslin
1 teaspoon sea salt
1 tablespoon granulated sugar
½ teaspoon ground cumin
½ teaspoon ground coriander
2 cloves
125 ml/4 fl oz/ ½ cup extra-
    virgin olive oil
65 ml/2 fl oz/¼ cup white
    wine vinegar
1 tablespoon Kirsch
    – optional

worth doing, pack the fruit and vegetables in preserving jars, five or six 400 g/14 oz jars should do it, and top with the sweet pickling vinegar on p.28 instead of the spices, olive oil, wine vinegar in the recipe, and remove the bundle of lavender after 3 or 4 days.

Pickled samphire

Samphire is one of my favourite seasonal treats, ever since I picked a bundle on the north Norfolk coast many years ago. Recipes for samphire have appeared in many of my newspaper columns and books and this is based on another in my *Times Cookbook*.

Pickled samphire has been a classic English preserve for centuries, usually prepared by leaving it in a low oven overnight covered in vinegar. I think that spoils the wonderful bright colour and crisp texture, producing a soft, khaki pickle, so instead I always use cold vinegar for mine.

Pick over the samphire, discarding any roots and soggy pieces. Rinse very thoroughly to get rid of any sand, and gently towel dry. Put the samphire in a glass bowl and sprinkle with the salt. Leave overnight, loosely covered. Next day, drain off any liquid and pack the samphire into sterilised jars together with the flowers. Cover completely with the vinegar, seal, and label. This is ready to use within a few days, but it will keep for months in a cool dry place.

Cook's tip

If you prefer, you can use a plain pickling vinegar instead of the sweet one. I use fennel or elderflowers, because sometimes the elderflowers last long enough to see the first of the samphire harvest.

makes 1 kg/2 lbs

1 kg/2 lbs samphire
175 g/6 oz/¾ cup coarse salt
6 fennel flower or elderflower
    heads – see recipe
750 ml-1 litre/1 ¼ – 1 ¾
    pint/3 to 4 cups sweet
    pickling vinegar (p.28)

Garden vegetable pickle

For those who love a certain 'brand' of pickle, here is a home-made version. With its double dose of vinegar, this pickle keeps particularly well in hot climates, and it is a recipe I developed when I was guest chef at British embassies in Cairo and Kuwait. You can, of course, vary the vegetables according to what you have available, adding pumpkin, aubergine, and small squash. You can also add chilli or ginger for an extra bite, but this would rather overpower the flowers.

Make a standard cold brine of 500 g/1 lb/ 2 cups of salt dissolved in 4 litres/7 pints/4 US quarts of water and cover the vegetables with it for 24 hours. Drain well and cover with the *unspiced* vinegar for 24 hours. Drain the vegetables again.

Mix the sugar, mustard, flour, turmeric, and allspice to a paste with a little of the spiced vinegar in a saucepan, gradually stirring in the rest of the vinegar until smooth. Put in the vegetables and the bundle of flowers and simmer for 20 minutes. Remove from the heat, discard the bundle of flowers and pot the pickle in hot, sterilised jars, seal and label.

makes about 3 kg/6 lbs

500 g/1 lb/2 cups cucumber, peeled, quartered lengthwise, seeds removed, and diced
500 g/1 lb/2 cups peeled and onions
500 g/1 lb/2 cups diced green tomatoes
500 g/1 lb/2 cups seedless raisins or sultanas
500 g/1 lb/2 cups diced French beans
500 g/1 lb/2 cups diced celery
500 g/1 lb/2 cups peeled and diced carrots
500 g/1 lb/2 cups salt
2 litres/3 ½ pints/2 US quarts malt vinegar
250 g/8 oz/1 cup dark muscovado or dark brown sugar
3 tablespoons mustard powder
2 tablespoons flour
1 tablespoon ground turmeric
2 teaspoons ground allspice
1 litre/1 ¾ pint/4 cups spiced vinegar, i.e. pickling vinegar
½ teaspoon lavender flowers and 6 fennel flower heads, tied in muslin

Spanish peppers with lavender

The recipe owes its name to the colours of the Spanish flag, and the fact that I generally serve these peppers with other Iberian ingredients. I find that green peppers are not worth preserving in this way, as they are not as fleshy as the red and yellow ones.

Quarter the peppers and remove seeds and pith, as well as the stalk. Place on a rack and grill until the peppers are soft and the skin charred and blistered, about 15 minutes. You can also roast them in a hot oven (200°C/400°F/gas mark 6) until cooked to the same point. Tip the pieces into a bowl, cover with cling film and let them cool. Peel the peppers and cut into wide strips or squares. Put them in a bowl with the rest of the ingredients, mix well and anoint liberally with olive oil. Cover and leave to marinate for 4 or 5 hours at room temperature.

Make sure the jars are sterilised and dried and fill with the peppers to 1 cm/½ inches from the rim. Add the vinegar, making sure the jar is completely full. Close with new rubber seals, also sterilised. Sterilise the jars of peppers for 40 minutes at 100°C/212°F using the method on p.33.

When cool, label and store in the pantry or other dark place. The peppers will keep for a year, and are excellent served with roast pork, as part of a tapas selection, with cold meats, or in a *pisto manchego* or Basque *pipérade*.

makes three 400 g/14 oz jars

4 large red peppers
4 large yellow peppers
1 teaspoon black peppercorns
1 teaspoon pink peppercorns
1 teaspoon coriander seeds
1 teaspoon sea salt
4 sprigs fresh lavender
7 tablespoons extra-virgin
   olive oil
Sherry vinegar – see recipe

Preserved lemons with fennel flowers

The lemons are an indispensable ingredient in Moroccan and other North African dishes, such as chicken and lemon tagine, carrot salad, and spiced grilled fish.

Cut down a lemon in quarters lengthways, without cutting right through. Put 2 teaspoons of salt in the cavity formed and place it in the jar right away. Continue with the remaining lemons and place these in the jar, interspersed with fennel flowers. Seal the jar and keep in a cool dry place. After about 3 weeks, the briny juice rendered should cover the lemons completely. If necessary, press them down with a wooden spoon.

fills one 1 kg/2 lbs/1 US quart jar

6 unwaxed, unsprayed lemons
12 teaspoons sea salt
6 to 8 fennel flower heads

Cook's tip

Fennel flowers can be replaced to very good effect with two or three lavender flowers.

Pickled artichokes and fennel flowers

My friend, Mary Grace, in Gozo, uses the local artichokes, of which one sees fields and fields in winter and early spring, to make these delicate pickles. I added the fennel flowers as fennel grows wild at the same time of year and brings its own subtle hint of anise.

Artichokes discolour quickly when cut surfaces are exposed to the air, so have a bowl of water with a generous splash of lemon juice into which you drop each artichoke as you prepare it. Remove the outer leaves from the artichokes and put them the acidulated water. When all are prepared, drain them and put them in a glass or plastic bowl. Mix the salt and water, pour over

makes 1 kg/2 lbs/1 US quart

1 kg/2 lbs baby artichokes
250 g/8 oz/1 cup salt
1 litre/4 cups water
500 ml/17 fl oz/2 cups white wine vinegar
250 ml/8 fl oz/1 cup white wine
2 tablespoons fennel seeds
1 tablespoon white peppercorns
250 g/8 oz/1 cup granulated sugar
6 to 8 fennel flower heads
75 ml/3 fl oz/⅓ cup olive oil

the artichokes, cover the bowl loosely with a clean tea towel and leave for 24 hours.

Meanwhile boil the vinegar, wine, fennel seeds, peppercorns, and sugar and put to one side.

Rinse the artichokes and put them in a nonreactive saucepan with this sweet spiced vinegar. Bring to the boil and boil the artichokes for 2 to 3 minutes, until just softening but not cooked through. Drop in the fennel flowers. Remove the pan from the heat. Pack the artichokes and flowers into sterilised hot preserving jars, with nonreactive lids. Shake the jars to ensure there are no air bubbles, topping up with vinegar if necessary. Make sure the artichokes are submerged in the liquid then float a layer of olive oil on top. Seal and label the jars. Try to keep for a month before using.

Cook's tip

Serve the artichokes as part of an antipasto or mezze, with olives, sun-dried tomatoes, pickled shallots, and a selection of salamis and cured meats.

Sweet cucumber and fennel pickles

This pickle is very simple to make, better than most you can buy, and is the classic accompaniment to a home-made burger.

Select firm, stiff cucumbers; any that wobble when you pick them up and lightly shake them are old and will be bitter and rubbery. A good cucumber will be moist, juicy, and crisp inside, with a good proportion of flesh to seed.

The cucumber is 96 per cent water, so the key to preserving them is to get rid as much of

makes 2 kg/4 lbs/2 US quarts

5 or 6 cucumbers

125 g/4 oz/½ cup salt

750 ml/1 ¼ pint/3 cups cider vinegar

6 to 8 fennel flower heads

500 g/2 cups granulated sugar

2 tablespoons fennel seeds

that water as possible, which you do by salting them. It is also a good idea to remove the watery core and seeds.

Halve the cucumbers lengthwise, and with an apple corer or teaspoon scrape out and discard the core of seeds. Cut the cucumbers into 1 cm/½ inch slices and put them in a glass or plastic bowl. Mix in the salt, cover the bowl loosely with a clean tea towel, and leave for 24 hours. Meanwhile boil the vinegar, sugar, and fennel seeds and put to one side.

Rinse and dry the cucumber pieces and pack them into the two jars, sterilised and still warm. Distribute fennel flowers amongst the cucumber pieces then pour on the sweet fennel-flavoured vinegar, including the seeds. Shake the jars to ensure there are no air bubbles, topping up with vinegar if necessary. Make sure the cucumber is submerged in the liquid, then seal and label the jars. Try to keep for a month before using.

Lavender pickled shallots

When chopping shallots and mixing with vinegar to serve with oysters, I once used lavender vinegar, which I found to be such a good combination that I always use it now, and from that developed the lavender pickled shallots. I like to use banana shallots for this because of their shape, but round ones work just as well. And, of course, the recipe works well with pickling onions.

Put the shallots in a bowl with half the salt and half the water and leave for 2 days. Drain them and repeat the process with the rest of the salt and

makes 1 kg/2 lbs/1 US quart

1 kg/2 lb shallots, peeled
375 g/12 oz/1 ½ cups salt
2 litres/1 ¾ pint/2 US quarts water
1 litre/1 ¾ pint/4 cups distilled malt vinegar
500 ml/17 fl oz/2 cups white wine vinegar
250 g/8 oz/1 cup sugar
4 or 5 lavender heads

water, and leave for 2 days. Drain them and cover with the malt vinegar, and again leave for 2 days.

Meanwhile, boil the white wine vinegar and sugar and put to one side. Drain the steeped shallots and pack them into a large preserving jar with a nonreactive lid. Tuck in the lavender and pour over the sweet vinegar. Shake the jar to ensure there are no air bubbles, topping up with more vinegar if necessary. Seal and label the jar, and leave for a month to mature.

Cook's tip

If you prefer, you can make the pickle without sugar, simply covering the shallots with plain wine vinegar.

Saffron pickled onions

Serve this with a traditional farmhouse Cheddar and some crusty bread, for a traditional English "ploughman's lunch."

Put the onions, unpeeled, in a nonreactive bowl, and add half the water and salt. Stir a few times to ensure that the salt dissolves. Leave, covered, for 24 hours. Drain the onions, peel them and put in the bowl with the remaining salt and water, leaving them for 24 hours. Meanwhile, bring the vinegar to the boil, with the saffron. Remove from the heat and allow to it to cool. Remove the onions from the brine and rinse thoroughly. Pack them in sterilised jars, with nonreactive lids, cover with the saffron vinegar, ensuring that there are no air bubbles. Then seal and label the jars and try to leave for at least 2 months before using.

makes 1 kg/2 lbs/1 US quart

1 kg/2 lbs pickling onions
2 litres/3 ½ pints/2 US quarts water
250 g/8 oz/1 cup salt
350 ml/¾ pint/1 ½ cup white wine vinegar
Generous pinch of saffron filaments

Cook's tip

You can use other floral vinegars to make these pickles. Shallots pickled with elderflower vinegar are very good.

Sweet fennel and orange pickle

Simmer the fennel in the sweet vinegar and orange juice in a nonreactive saucepan for 30 minutes. Remove the pan from the heat, stir in the orange flower water, and leave the contents to cool. Once cool, remove the fennel from the pan and pack into hot sterilised jars, distributing the orange zest. Re-boil the vinegar and strain it through a small strainer over the fennel, covering them by 5 cm/ 2 inches. Seal and label the jars and leave for a week or two for the flavour to mature.

fills four 250 g/8 oz jars

1 kg/2 lbs miniature fennel, left whole, or 2 or 3 large Florence fennel bulbs, cut into wedges

250 ml/8 fl oz/1 cup fresh orange juice

750 ml/1 ¼ pint/3 cups sweet pickling vinegar (p. 28)

1 to 2 tablespoons orange flower water

Thinly pared zest of 2 oranges

Lavender pickled pears

Put all the ingredients, except the pears, in a saucepan. Heat the mixture gently until the sugar has dissolved and then bring to the boil.

Meanwhile, quarter, peel, and core the pears, and place them in a large bowl. Pour the boiling liquid over them, cover, and leave overnight. Strain the liquid back into a saucepan and boil it for 10 to 12 minutes to reduce the volume since the pears will have given off some liquid. Pour the liquid over the fruit and allow to stand for half a day. Boil the fruit and syrup together for a minute, then remove the pan from the heat. With a perforated spoon, remove the pears, and pack into hot, sterilised preserving jars.

fills three or four 1 kg/ 2 lbs/1 US quart jars

500 ml/17 fl oz/2 cups red wine vinegar

750 g/1 ½ lbs/3 cups granulated sugar

1 cinnamon stick, broken into 3 or 4 pieces

12 allspice berries

12 cloves

2 or 3 myrtle leaves

1 bay leaf

6 to 8 sprigs of fresh lavender

10 Bosc pears or another firm variety

Re-boil the syrup, pour it over the pears, distributing the spices between the jars and seal the jars immediately. Allow to cool, label, and store. Keep for at least 3 weeks before using.

Spiced lavender pickled peaches

These are excellent with pork and pale game meats such as pheasant and quail, and also perfect with a whole cooked ham.

Blanch the peaches in boiling water, refresh under cold running water, then remove the skin. Halve the peaches, discard the stones, and stick a sprig of lavender in each half. Put the peaches and the rest of the ingredients in a nonreactive saucepan and heat gently until the sugar has dissolved. Bring to the boil and simmer for 4 minutes. Transfer the fruit with a perforated spoon to a sterilised preserving jar or jars, letting any juice run back into the pan. Boil the liquid for about 10 minutes, until thickened, and pour over the peaches. Seal and label the jar.

makes two 1 kg/2 lbs/1 US quart jars

8 firm but ripe peaches
16 sprigs of lavender
500 g/1 lb/2 cups granulated sugar
1 cinnamon stick
8 crushed cardamom pods
500 ml/17 fl oz/2 cups white wine vinegar

Melon and lime flower pickle

This is a very delicate, fragrant pickle. If lime flowers are not available, you can use jasmine or elderflowers.

Halve and quarter the melon, discard the rind and seeds, and cut the flesh into cubes. This is less wasteful than scooping the melon into balls. Put the chunks in a large bowl, sprinkle on the salt, and pour on the water. Stir a few times to dissolve the salt then

makes four 400 g/14 oz jars

1 green or yellow-fleshed melon such as honeydew or Galia, of about 1 kilo/2 lbs in weight
125 g/4 oz/½ cup salt
1 litre/1 ¾ pint/4 cups water
500 ml/17 fl oz/2 cups sweet vinegar – see p.28

place a plate on top of the fruit to keep it submerged in the brine. Leave for 24 hours, drain, and then put into a nonreactive saucepan with the vinegar and lime flowers. Simmer for 3 or 4 minutes and remove from the heat. Transfer the melon into steril- ised preserving jars with a slotted spoon, dispersing the lime flowers amongst the pieces of fruit, cover with the vinegar, and seal and label the jars.

3 to 4 sprigs lime (linden) flowers

Roasted tomato, fennel, and red pepper pickle

Quarter the smaller fennel bulbs, or cut the large one into 8 wedges depending on size and shape, brush with olive oil, and place on a grill rack or baking sheet. Quarter the peppers and tomatoes, discard the seeds, and add to the fennel. Grill or roast all the vegetables for about 10 to 15 minutes. The fennel will still be relatively firm. Skin the peppers and tomatoes when cool enough to do so. Then put the vegetables in a bowl, sprinkle on the salt, cover, and refrigerate or keep in a cool place for 24 to 36 hours.

Meanwhile, prepare the vinegar. Since it is already spiced, it does not need long cooking. Put in a saucepan with the spices and sugar. Heat it gently until the sugar has dissolved and then boil for 2 minutes. Cool. Rinse the vege- tables thoroughly. Drain and dry them, and pack in to sterilised preserving jars. Distribute the fennel flowers among the vegetables. Fill the jars with the cold strained vinegar, seal, label, and store it for a couple of weeks before using.

makes about 1 kg/2 lbs/ 1 US quart

1 large or two smaller fennel bulbs, about 500 g/1 lb, altogether
Extra-virgin olive oil – see recipe
2 sweet red peppers
4 large plum tomatoes
125 g/4 oz/½ cup salt
500 ml/ 17 fl oz/2 cups distilled malt pickling vinegar
1 teaspoon coriander seeds
1 teaspoon fennel seeds
8 crushed cardamom pods
250 g/8 oz/1 cup granulated sugar
8 to 10 fennel flowers

Fennel pickled walnuts

For those lucky enough to have their own tree, pick the walnuts still green when the kernel is full and white, but before the shell hardens. This method for pickling walnuts is based on a recipe from the seventeenth-century English gardener and scholar John Evelyn. The sharp, salty flavour of this very traditional pickle is excellent with cold meats or cheese, or with a slice of coarse country terrine.

Put the walnuts in a nonreactive pan, cover with water, and bring to the boil. The water will blacken, drain the walnuts, cover with fresh water, and boil once more. Continue until the water remains clear. Put the walnuts in a bowl of water for 2 days, renewing the water several times. Drain and dry carefully in a clean tea towel. Put the walnuts in preserving jars, layered with the salt and aromatics, until the jar is three-quarters full. Use a spoonful of salt for each layer of walnuts. Fill with vinegar; sherry vinegar will make this into a most luxurious condiment. Seal and leave for 3 months. Home-pickled walnuts make an excellent present.

makes 1 kg/2 lbs/1 US quart

1 kg/2 lbs fresh green walnuts
125 g/4 oz/½ cup salt
1 teaspoon fennel seed
1 teaspoon black peppercorns
1 teaspoon blade mace or sliced nutmeg
6 to 8 fennel flower heads
About 500 ml/17 fl oz/2 cups vinegar – see recipe

Elderflower vinegar

This is one of my favourite vinegars, with a myriad uses, from simple salad dressings, to flavouring a mayonnaise or sauce to serve with fish and shellfish.

Shake the flowers to remove any insects or loose pollen and put them in a large glass pitcher or jar with the vinegar. Stand the

makes 2 litres/3 ½ pints/2 US quarts

2 litres/3 ½ pint/2 US quarts white wine vinegar
12 to 18 elderflower heads, plus extra
– see recipe

pitcher on a sunny window sill and leave for 1 week or so. After that time, strain the vinegar into clean bottles, and put a sprig of fresh elderflowers in each bottle. Seal the bottles, label, and store in a dark place. If you still have the vinegar next year, remove the old flowers and add fresh ones.

Raspberry and lavender vinegar

Use this to deglaze the pan after cooking calf's liver or chicken livers for a subtle and unique taste sensation.

Put the raspberries and 4 lavender flowers in a large nonreactive bowl and pour the vinegar over them. Crush with a potato masher, cover the bowl, and leave to infuse for 1 or 2 days. Strain into a jug through a sieve lined with muslin, and then pour into sterilised bottles. Enhance the lavender flavour by inserting a head of lavender in each bottle. Seal and label them.

makes about 1.5 litres/2 ½ pints/1 ½ US quart

1 kg/2 lbs raspberries
8 lavender flower heads – see recipe
1 litre/1 ¾ pint/4 cups white wine vinegar

Provençal vinegar

For dressing a *salade niçoise*, combined with extra-virgin olive oil from the same region, this vinegar is full of the flavours of the *garrigue*.

Take a heatproof glass jug, large enough to take all the ingredients and the liquid, and in it put the onions and garlic, all the herbs and flowers, first briefly rinsed and carefully dried, and the peppercorns. Put the vinegar in a nonreactive saucepan and bring to the boil. Pour it into the jug and allow it to cool. Cover it loosely enough to let air circulate – pierced cling film works

makes 1 litre/1 ¾ pint/ 1 US quart

1 large mild onion, peeled and sliced
10 cloves of garlic, peeled
12 stalks of basil
12 stalks of parsley
2 or 3 sprigs thyme
6 lavender heads on the stalk
4 stalks of leaf fennel in flower– or a quarter fennel bulb, sliced

perfectly – and leave for 2 weeks in a cool dry place. Filter the vinegar and decant into smaller bottles; I like to use 250 ml/8 fl oz bottles. Seal and label the bottles.

2 bay leaves
2 sprigs of thyme
1 tablespoon pink peppercorns
1 litre/1 ¾ pint/4 cups white wine vinegar

Violet vinegar

The flowers are so subtly scented that you need the palest, mildest vinegar you can find. I like to use coconut vinegar, which you will find wherever Filipino goods are sold, or a mild Japanese rice vinegar. Some supermarket white wine vinegars will also do, as they are very bland. Cider vinegar is too dark, and too distinctive in flavour.

4 or 5 handfuls violet flowers
750 ml/1 ¼ pint/3 cups vinegar – see below

Put the flowers only, all green parts removed, into a glass jug. Pour on the vinegar. Seal the top of the jug with pierced cling film and place somewhere sunny. Leave for 1 week or so for the scent and colour to transfer to the vinegar. Strain and bottle in fairly small bottles, 200 ml/7 oz, then cork and label. Keep the vinegar in a dark place so that it will retain its colour. Even so, the colour, and indeed the flavour will gradually fade. You can help it out with a dash of violet syrup.

This is the vinegar to use when preparing mild leaf salads garnished with edible flowers such as borage, pansies, clove carnation, and rose petals.

Cook's tip

Apply the same method to purple pansies, and make a delicately coloured and faintly scented vinegar. Violets are more fragrant than purple pansies, which have only a very faint scent, but the colour obtained in a pansy vinegar is so pretty that it is worth the trouble harvesting a few of these good-tempered spring garden flowers.

Wild garlic flower vinegar

Of all the onion family, this makes the most delicately flavoured vinegar, and with a sprig of wild garlic in the bottle, it looks too elegant to want to hide in a dark pantry. For this reason, I usually bottle this in 250 ml/8 fl oz bottles, the one in which some white wine vinegars are sold.

Shake the flowers to remove any insects and put them in a large glass jug or jar with the vinegar and cover with pierced cling film. Stand the jug on a sunny window sill and leave for 1 week or so, stirring from time to time. Strain the vinegar into clean bottles, and put a sprig of fresh flowers in each bottle. Seal the bottles, label, and store in a dark place. If you still have the vinegar next year, remove the old flowers and add fresh ones, as described on p.136.

makes 1 litre/1 ¾ pint/1 US quart

1 litre/1 ¾ pint/4 cups white wine vinegar
10 wild garlic flowers, kept on 10 cm/4 inches of stalk, plus
extra – see recipe

Kiwi, elderflower, and jalapeño ketchup

The ketchup is a very versatile condiment, excellent with grilled or barbecued poultry or fish, and also a useful ingredient to paint on before grilling. It is very good too, as an accompaniment to smoked fish, especially mackerel and swordfish.

In a nonreactive pan simmer the shallots in 1 tablespoon of water until almost tender, then add the kiwi flesh, the jalapeño, black pepper and juniper, and simmer for 30 minutes or so. Add the vinegar and sugar and cook for about 15 minutes, until the mixture thickens. Remove the pan from the heat. When cool, sieve or blend the ketchup

makes about two 250 g/ 8 oz jars

6 shallots, chopped
6 moderately ripe kiwis, peeled and diced
1 or 2 jalapeño peppers, halved, seeded, and thinly sliced
½ teaspoon ground black pepper
½ teaspoon ground juniper
250 ml/8 fl oz/1 cup elderflower vinegar (p.137)
250 g/8 oz/1 cup granulated sugar

until smooth. Pour into jars or bottles, seal, and label. If you like, store the ketchup in the refrigerator in squeeze bottles with nozzles. This way, if a simple dollop will not suffice, you can splash and swirl the ketchup on the plate.

Cook's tip

In many of my pickle and chutney recipes, I recommend one of the raw or unrefined sugars, but in this case I recommend white sugar, as otherwise the kiwi cooks to a less than appetizing khaki colour. Indeed, it is one of the few recipes where I would consider using a dash of food colouring to keep a true green.

If you wish to keep the ketchup for several months, then you should process it in a hot water bath, following the method on p.33.

Tomato and lavender ketchup

This is a ketchup to make in high summer when tomatoes are at their ripest, and lavender and basil ready for picking. It gives an intriguing note to the sauces used for seafood. Marie Rose sauce has the ketchup mixed with mayonnaise; cocktail sauce, for the classic prawn cocktail, is made with ketchup mixed with a little horseradish.

Simmer the onion in 1 tablespoon of water until almost tender, then add the roughly chopped tomatoes and as much juice as you have been able to retain, as well as the basil and lavender, and simmer for 30 minutes or so. Add the seasoning, the vinegar, and sugar, and cook for 15 minutes or until the mixture thickens. Remove the pan from the

makes about 1 kg/2 lbs/ 4 cups

1 medium onion, peeled and finely chopped

2 kg/4 lbs ripe tomatoes

Several sprigs of fresh basil

1 teaspoon lavender flowers

½ teaspoon salt

½ teaspoon freshly ground black pepper

250 ml/8 fl oz/1 cup vinegar – cider, white wine or distilled

250 g/8 oz/1 cup light brown sugar

heat. When cool, blend the ketchup until smooth and sieve it as the tomatoes were not peeled. Pour into jars or bottles, seal, and label.

Cook's tip

If you wish to keep the ketchup in your pantry for several months, you should process it in a water bath, following the method on p.33.

Mango, ginger, and jasmine ketchup

Like the kiwi, elderflower, and jalapeño ketchup on p.139, this versatile preserve can be used in cooking as well as an accompaniment to cooked meat and fish, or on sandwiches. It is particularly good with seafood, such as barbecued or grilled prawns.

Simmer the onion in 1 tablespoon of water until almost tender, then add the mango flesh and as much juice as you have been able to retain, as well as the cumin, ginger, cinnamon, and jasmine, and simmer for 30 minutes or so. Add the vinegar and sugar and cook for 15 minutes or until the mixture thickens. Remove the pan from the heat. Discard the cinnamon stick. When cool, sieve, or blend the ketchup until smooth. Pour into jars or bottles, seal, and label.

makes about 750 g/1½ lb/ 3 cups

1 medium onion, peeled and finely chopped

3 or 4 ripe mangoes, peeled and diced

1 teaspoon ground cumin

1 teaspoon freshly grated ginger

1 cinnamon stick

3 heaping tablespoons jasmine flowers

250 ml/8 fl oz/1 cup vinegar – cider, white wine, or distilled

250 g/8 oz/1 cup light brown sugar

Cook's tip

If you wish to keep the ketchup in your pantry for several months, you should process it in a boiling water bath, following the method on p.33.

Elderberry ketchup

Elderberries are best combined with blackberries (see p.70) in a hedgerow jelly, but are also the basis of a traditional English condiment, Pontac sauce, spicy, peppery, and robust in flavour, which is very good with roast or grilled lamb and dark game meats such as venison or hare. The hint of lavender works very well with the punchy spices.

Remove the berries from the stalks, put in an ovenproof bowl or large preserving jar, and pour the boiling vinegar over the fruit. Leave it in the oven overnight, with the oven set to very low, 100°F/50°C. Strain the liquid into a nonreactive saucepan, mashing the elderberries to release their pulp, and boil it for 5 minutes with the salt, sugar, peppercorns, cloves, lavender, and shallots. Allow to cool completely, then pour into sterilised bottles, seal, and label.

makes about 500 ml/ 17 fl oz/2 cups

500 g/1 lb ripe elderberries
500 ml/17 fl oz/2 cups red wine vinegar
1 teaspoon salt
125 g/4 oz/½ cup granulated sugar
1 tablespoon black peppercorns
10 cloves
½ teaspoon dried culinary lavender flowers
4 shallots, peeled and finely chopped

Tomatillo and fennel flower salsa

A member of the *Physalis* family and resembling pale green tomatoes with a papery husk, tomatillos are also called husk tomatoes. Originating in Mexico, they are much used there in salsas and other savoury dishes. Since their introduction far beyond Mexico's borders – London farmers' markets have them in summer – their use has extended to a wider range of relishes and preserves, including jams and ketchups. When ripe, the fruit turns a very pale yellow and bursts out of its light brown husk.

makes about four 250 g/ 8 oz jars

1 kg/2 lbs tomatillos, husks removed
1 tart apple, peeled and cored
2 large onions, chopped
2 or 3 green chillies, sliced (seeds and membranes removed)
2 or 3 cloves garlic, peeled and sliced
250 g/8 oz/1 cup granulated sugar

This is a lightly cooked salsa, pale green, subtly flavoured and refreshing, and perfect with seared scallops or sautéed prawns.

Roughly chop the tomatillos and apple and put in nonreactive pan with the onion, chillies, garlic, and sugar. Combine the lime juice and white wine with the wine vinegar to 500 ml/17 fl oz/2 cups and add to the pan. Mix well, bring to the boil and simmer for 1 hour until the mixture has thickened. Add the fennel flowers, mix well, and remove the pan from the heat. Pot the salsa in hot, sterilised jars with nonreactive lids, seal, and label. For keeping more than a couple of months, process following the water bath method on p.33.

Juice of 4 limes
125 ml/4 fl oz/½ cup white wine
White wine vinegar – see recipe
8 to 10 fennel flower heads

Mango, jasmine, and yellow tomato salsa

This bright and lively salsa is an excellent accompaniment to all Mexican-inspired dishes, and many others, fish as well as meat. It is excellent with grilled prawns and griddled scallops, for example.

Peel and dice the mango. Halve and seed the tomatoes, and chop the flesh. Peel and finely chop the shallot. Heat the oil in a frying pan, add the mango, tomato, chilli, and shallot and cook until soft and cooked through. Trim and thinly slice the spring onion and stir into the mixture, together with the jasmine flowers, sugar, vinegar, and salt, and cook gently for about 15 minutes. Remove the pan from the heat. Spoon the salsa into hot sterilised jars, seal, and label.

Cook's tip

If you wish to keep the salsa in your pantry for several months, you should process it in a boiling water bath, following the method on p.33.

makes about 500 g/1 lb/ 2 cups

2 moderately ripe mangoes
4 yellow tomatoes
2 shallots
1 yellow Scotch Bonnet or milder chilli, seeded and sliced
2 tablespoons rapeseed oil
2 or 3 spring onions
2 heaped tablespoons jasmine flowers
2 tablespoons light brown sugar
3 tablespoons white wine vinegar
½ teaspoon salt

Lavender-scented tomato salsa

This recipe is based on the classic salsa found in Mexican restaurants, piquant and full of ripe flavours. It is only worth making in high summer when tomatoes are at their peak of perfection, and the lavender, which is, of course, not traditional, in full bloom.

Put all the ingredients in a large nonreactive pan and bring the mixture to a boil, stirring frequently. Reduce the heat and simmer for 20 minutes, stirring occasionally. Ladle the hot salsa into sterilised jars, leaving 2 cm/½ inches headspace. Adjust the lids and process in a boiling water bath for 15 minutes following the method on p.33. Label and store the jars for at least a couple of weeks before using, to allow the flavours to develop.

makes eight 250 g/8 oz jars

1.5 kg/3 lbs peeled, cored, and chopped tomatoes

2 red or green peppers, seeded and chopped

2 jalapeño peppers, seeded and sliced

2 shallots, peeled and chopped

4 cloves garlic, finely chopped

500 ml/17 fl oz/2 cups red or white wine vinegar

1 teaspoon lavender buds

1 tablespoon fresh coriander, chopped

1 ½ teaspoons salt

Yellow tomato, fennel, mint, and sweet corn salsa

This is a lively and colourful alternative to a classic tomato salsa. It is fabulous with a home-made hamburger, or a grilled skirt steak.

Gently fry the onion until soft, and then add the tomatoes and chilli. Raise the heat, and add the apple juice. Cook the vegetables until just soft, then add the vinegar, sugar, fennel flowers, mint, salt, pepper, and the corn. Continue cooking for 30 minutes or until the mixture has thickened, then remove the pan from the heat. Pour the salsa into hot, sterilised jars, and process them for 15 minutes in a boiling water bath, following the method on p.33. Label and store the jars for at least a couple of

makes about 1 kg/2 lbs/ 4 cups

1 large mild onion, peeled and chopped

1 tablespoon sunflower oil

500 g/1 lb yellow tomatoes, halved, seeded, and chopped

1 or more green or red chillies, seeded, and finely chopped

125 ml/4 fl oz/½ cup apple juice

250 ml/8 fl oz/1 cup cider vinegar

weeks before using, to allow the flavours to develop.

250 g/8 oz/1 cup granulated
   sugar
4 tablespoons fresh fennel
   flowers, roughly chopped
2 tablespoons fresh mint,
   chopped
1 teaspoon salt
1 ¼ teaspoons pepper
4 ears fresh sweet corn,
   kernels removed

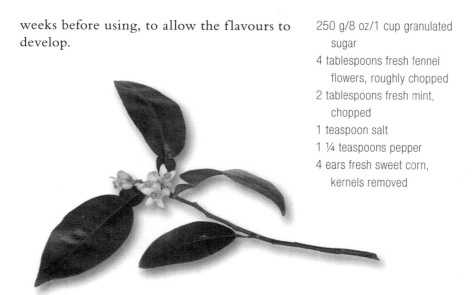

Cranberry, kumquat, and orange flower salsa

This is a quickly made salsa for winter when cranberries and mandarins are in season, and the orange flower water brings with it a gentle fragrance.

Halve the kumquats, discard the seeds, and quarter the fruit. Partially cover the pan with its lid and cook the onion, garlic, kumquats, and cranberries in the mandarin juice until the cranberries have popped. Stir in the sugar and once it has dissolved, boil until the mixture thickens. Towards the end of cooking, add a little salt, about ½ teaspoon and a grinding of pepper, as well as the orange flower water. Remove the pan from the heat. Spoon the salsa into sterilised, hot jars, seal, and label. If you want to keep the salsa for more than 2 or 3 weeks, process it following the water bath method on p.33.

**makes about two 250 g/
8 oz jars**

8 kumquats
1 onion, chopped
2 garlic cloves, peeled and
   crushed
Juice of 2 to 3 mandarins
350 g/12 oz fresh or frozen
   cranberries
175 g/6 oz/1 cup lightly
   packed soft brown sugar
Salt
Pepper
1 to 2 tablespoons orange
   flower water

Fire and ice

In this chapter, as well as salt, sugar, and vinegar, I use fire
and ice for preserving food with floral flavours. The fiery
heat of a hot summer's day – or several – is what you need
to achieve perfect sun-dried tomatoes and figs, as well as
the rich, dark tomato paste made from a glut of Mediterranean tomatoes. Fortunately, in the absence of sun, a
well-regulated oven will produce almost indistinguishable
results.

Smoking is another ancient method for preserving food
which, like many others, has been overtaken by refrigera-
tion. But we still like the flavour of smoked food, although
a very light touch is normally used nowadays. And most of it
is cold-smoked, a long, technical process outside the scope of
this book. Fragrance in the form of fennel or lavender stalks
can be added when hot-smoking salmon, for example, but
that is a cooking method rather than a preserving one. For
those lucky enough to be able to cold-smoke a side or two of
salmon, however, do experiment with adding fragrance to
the wood chips, in the form of jasmine tea and extra jasmine
flowers, as well as fennel and lavender.

Another way of preserving the scent of flowers is, of
course, to freeze them. One of my earliest floral recipes
was to capture and preserve the glorious scent of a hot

summer in rose petal ice cream and lavender sorbet, and freezing certainly preserves these scents beautifully. Although ice creams and sorbets keep for a long time in the freezer, the fragrance gradually fades, so I recommend you not to keep them for longer than a month or so. When fresh scented edible flowers are not available, dried ones can be used, or you can use floral syrups.

The scent and flavour of flowers can also be preserved in oils, butters, and even mustards, as in the following selection of recipes.

Goat cheese with lemon, lavender, and chilli

This makes a lovely present, and is also a very good item to have on hand for an instant first course.

Rinse and dry the lemon and slice it. Place on a plate and sprinkle each piece with about ½ teaspoon salt. Cover with cling film and leave to macerate for 24 hours. Rinse well under running water and leave in a plastic sieve for 2 hours. Dry the slices thoroughly on kitchen paper.

In a sterilised and dried preserving jar, pack in the cheeses, alternating with the lemon slices, and sprinkle with the lavender flowers and chilli. Cover the cheese completely with olive oil, seal, and leave in the pantry or other cool, dark place for 10 days before using. Unopened, this will keep for a month. Once opened, refrigerate and use within 3 days.

fills one 1 kg/2 lbs/1 US quart container

1 lemon

coarse sea salt – see recipe

12 small fresh goat cheeses or equivalent in sliced goat cheese logs, about 600 g/ 24 oz

1 teaspoon lavender flowers

1 chilli, thinly sliced

extra-virgin olive oil – see recipe

Cook's tip

Put a piece of the marinated cheese on a thick slice of sourdough bread, toasted on one side, flash it under the grill until the cheese is just beginning to melt, and serve with a tender spinach salad. You can also use it to stuff vegetables for baking, spooning a little of the seasoned oil on top.

Lavender-scented sun-dried tomatoes

Drying is a particularly useful way of preserving tomatoes. They take up less room than jars, store extremely well, and in addition, make good presents. They have a dense texture and concentrated flavour which makes them an excellent ingredient for adding to slow-cooking casseroles.

My father showed me how to prepare these in the Maltese islands, where my parents went to live in the early 1980s, long before sun-dried tomatoes had become a fashionable ingredient. It was simply what everyone did with the abundance of tomatoes, sometimes three crops a year. We spread the halved tomatoes in shallow wooden fruit trays, sprinkled them with coarse, unrefined sea salt and left them in the sun all day, covered with fine mesh or muslin to protect them from insects. At sundown, we brought them indoors, as otherwise the dew would have undone all the sun's drying. As we put them out in the sun again next morning, we pressed each tomato lightly with a couple of fingers, bringing more moisture to the surface, which would evaporate by the end of the day. In high summer it takes 5 to 6 days for the tomatoes to become dry enough to pack, lightly oiled, in jars, which you then seal and label.

You can use a similar method for oven-drying. Place the tomatoes on a baking sheet, cut side up, sprinkled with salt and lavender, and leave

makes 24 pieces

12 plum or other intensely
  flavoured tomatoes, halved
3 to 4 lavender flower heads
  – see recipe
6 teaspoons coarse sea salt –
  see recipe
6 consecutive hot, sunny days
  – see recipe

them in the oven on its lowest setting until the tomatoes are dry and wrinkled, and no more moisture is to be seen in the middle. A fan oven is particularly suitable. Ideally, the temperature should be 45–50°C/115–120°F. Any higher than this and the tomatoes will begin to cook rather than dry. If your oven cannot be set as low as this, secure it in such a way that you can keep the door slightly ajar.

For each tomato half, whether sun- or oven-dried, you need a generous pinch of coarse sea salt and no more than 3 or 4 lavender flowers – not whole flower heads, but single buds or flowers. Proceed as described above. Clearly, 12 plum tomatoes is only a suggestion; if you are sun-drying, you may want to do several trays at once, as my neighbours on Gozo do. And if you are oven-drying, you can probably do two trays, in which case, double the quantity of tomatoes. With an electric dehydrator, simply follow the manufacturer's instructions.

Cook's tip

A very simple pasta sauce can be made by cutting sun-dried tomatoes into strips and tossing them with some crushed garlic and olive oil into a bowl of freshly cooked pasta.

Maltese *kunserva* with lavender

This is another preserve I learned from my Gozitan friends. During the summer months, traditionally before the feast of Santa Marija on 15 August, their mothers and grandmothers would prepare kilos of tomatoes which would be dried or turned into *polpo, passata,* and *kunserva.* Even today, the most modern households continue the tradition. *Hobz biz*

zejt u l'kunserva is the winter version of a
favourite Maltese summer snack, bread with
olive oil and tomatoes. Even in the Mediterranean, winter tomatoes have little flavour, so
instead the bread is spread with the dark and
richly flavoured *kunserva*. The lavender is my
addition; it works well with tomatoes.

If you should find yourself with heroic quantities of tomatoes – it will take 10 kilos to make
barely 1 kilo of *kunserva* – plenty of time, and
hot sunny days, here is how to make it. The
idea is to concentrate the tomato flavour,
so the best way is to halve the tomatoes and
scoop out the seeds and liquid into a sieve
set over a bowl. After a few hours, you will
have fragrant tomato water to use for another
recipe – the vodka on p.112 perhaps? Roughly
chop the halved tomatoes and put them in 1
or 2 large stockpots. Add 1 to 2 teaspoons of
lavender tied in a muslin square and 1 heaping
tablespoon salt for 5 kilos/10 lbs of chopped
tomatoes. Cook for about 15 to 20 minutes,
then sieve the tomatoes into a large clean tray,
removing the lavender bag. Put the tray on a
table in the sun, cover with muslin and leave it
outdoors as long as the sun is hot. As with the
sun-dried tomatoes, bring it indoors before the
sun goes down, otherwise the dew will undo
all the sun's work. Do the same next day, and
the day after that, and so on until the paste is
dark and sticky. Each day, turn the mixture
with a spatula, to make sure that it is drying
evenly. When the *kunserva* is ready, pot it in
small sterilised jars and cover with a thin layer
of olive oil. Store in the fridge indefinitely
or in a cool dark pantry for 2 to 3 months.
Process in a water bath – see p.33 and the jars
will keep until next tomato season.

In the absence of hot sunny days, you can use an ovenproof tray and let the paste dry in a low oven until the same texture is reached; several hours instead of several days, but not nearly as much fun. In Malta and Sicily, where the same method is used, the tomato pulp is spread directly onto a scrubbed wooden table kept especially for the purpose.

Fragrant *mostarda*

Mostarda di frutta is a lovely Italian condiment traditionally served with *bollito misto* and cooked sausages such as *zampone* and *cotecchino*. It is also delicious with cold cuts and charcuterie. Lightly candied, the fruit is spiced with mustard, and in the following recipes, I have added an extra layer of flavour with some matching floral notes.

Pear, star anise, and fennel flower *mostarda*

Put all the ingredients except the pears in a stock pot or large saucepan, bring to the boil, stirring to dissolve the sugar, then add the pears. Simmer, stirring frequently, for 20 minutes. As the pears begin to soften, take care when stirring, so as not to break up the fruit – the slices look very attractive in the finished product. Continue to cook until the mixture thickens, as the liquid evaporates. This will take 45 minutes to 1 hour, and the mixture will need stirring from time to time to prevent it from sticking.

Pot the mixture in sterilised jars, seal, and label. The *mostarda* will keep for about 4 weeks in a cool, dark place, but for longer storage, you should process the jars using a water bath – see p.33.

makes about three 500 g/ 1 lb jars

1.5 kg/3 lbs pears, peeled, cored and sliced
750 ml/1 ¼ pints/3 cups water
750 ml/1 ¼ pints/3 cups white wine vinegar
500g/1 lb/2 cups light brown sugar
3 tablespoons English mustard powder
2 tablespoons Dijon mustard
2 tablespoons brown mustard seeds
2 teaspoons sea salt
3 star anise
1 tablespoon fennel flowers

Peach and lavender *mostarda*

Put all the ingredients except the peaches in a stock pot or large saucepan, bring to the boil, stirring to dissolve the sugar, then add the peaches. Simmer, stirring frequently, for 20 minutes. As the peaches begin to soften, mash them with a potato masher or back of your spoon to break up the larger pieces, but do not mash until smooth, as this is rather nicer with some texture. Continue to cook until the mixture thickens, as the liquid evaporates. This will take 45 minutes to 1 hour, and the mixture will need stirring from time to time to prevent it from sticking.

Pot the mixture in sterilised jars, seal, and label. The *mostarda* will keep for about 4 weeks in a cool, dark place, but for longer storage, you should process the jars using a water bath – see p.33.

makes about three 500 g/ 1 lb jars

1.5 kg/3 lbs peaches, stoned and chopped
750 ml/1 ¼ pints/3 cups water
750 ml/1 ¼ pints/3 cups cider vinegar
500g/1 lb/2 cups light brown sugar
3 tablespoons English mustard powder
2 tablespoons Dijon mustard
2 tablespoons brown mustard seeds
2 teaspoons sea salt
1 teaspoon lavender flowers

Myrtle-scented figs

If you are lucky enough to have access to plenty of fresh figs, this is a way to preserve them other than (see p.43). Myrtle has a wonderful, subtle scent, not unlike bay. You can, of course use bay leaves instead. Or try the same method using fennel flowers and seeds.

Many recipes instruct you to halve the figs to ensure quicker drying, but I prefer to keep them whole like the figs we buy in rectangular packs from Turkey.

The figs must be absolutely ripe, which is only at the point when they fall from the

3 kg/6 lb fresh fruit will make 1 kg/2 lbs dried fruit

Ripe figs – see recipe
Myrtle flowers and leaves – see recipe
A few hot, sunny days – see recipe

tree. This is why purchasing fresh figs from a greengrocer or supermarket often proves to be such a disappointment; they have been picked before they are ripe, and they do not ripen further after picking. This is, I know, is the case with so much fruit, but I regard figs as such a treat, and they are never cheap, that I want to eat them in perfect condition. My passion for the fruit stems from living in South Africa for a short time as a schoolgirl, where our garden, in the Cape wine country, had a fig tree growing outside the kitchen door.

So, once again, a method rather than a recipe. Rinse and dry the figs thoroughly. With a sharp knife, make a slit from the stalk to the base. Open it slightly. This will speed the drying process as the juices will be exposed to the air. Stick a myrtle leaf in each slit. Place the figs on a tray, scatter some myrtle flowers on and between them and, if drying outside, cover with muslin or other fine gauze to keep insects away. At sundown, bring the tray indoors. Put the figs out in the sun again next morning and press each one down lightly. It will take 2 to 3 days of hot sun for the figs to become dry enough to pack. Remove the myrtle flowers and leaves, and press the figs flat into a round. Place one on top of each other, with fresh myrtle leaves between each one. Wrap each roll of 6 to 8 figs in wax paper then in foil or cling film for storage. If properly dried, and stored in a cool dry place, they will keep until the next fig season.

If drying figs in the oven, set it at 45–50°C/115–120°F and leave the figs there until dry and wrinkled, somewhere in the region of 24 hours. A dehydrator can also be used, in which case follow the manufacturer's instructions.

Floral *Rumtopf*

The *Rumtopf* is a collection of fruit preserved in liqueur, very popular in continental Europe, often stored in specially made, decorative ceramic jars. A large, old-fashioned glass sweetie jar is a most acceptable substitute. The cherry is the fruit generally used to start the "rum pot."

My version is a floral *Rumtopf*, layering fruit, floral sugar, and white rum through the summer. The pot is then stoppered after the last fruit has been added, and saved for Christmas. I have given a blueprint recipe to start off the process, but it is more useful for me to give you a description, as the fruit and flowers will vary according to where you live.

It is essential to use ripe, but firm and undamaged fruit, with no sign of bruising or mould, as this will spoil the whole batch. You need a wide-neck jar, so that you can insert a small saucer to sit on top of the fruit and keep it submerged in the alcohol and sugar syrup.

Also called *confiture de vieux garçon*, or bachelor's jam, the best fruits to use, adding to it throughout the summer are cherries, both tart and sweet, apricots, nectarines, and peaches. Apricots should be halved and stoned. Peaches should be quartered. Red, black, and white currants are excellent, as are grapes, greengages, and plums later in the year. I do not find the softer fruit and berries respond well; so leave out strawberries and raspberries and their relations. For the floral sugar, I recommend rose, carnation, and jasmine, using the method on pp.25–26. These are all

1 kg/2 lbs cherries or apricots
1 litre/1 ¾ pint/1 US quart white rum
500 g/1 lb/2 cups floral scented sugar —see p.25

delicate scents, which are perfectly harmonious when used together. The addition of lavender would overpower the other flowers and I do not recommend it in this recipe. Using fresh flowers is less successful, as they look very dismal in the result, brown and wilted by the alcohol.

Build up your selection through the summer and autumn, and you will have an excellent jar of fruit in liqueur to serve as an instant dessert through the winter. Serve a spoonful of the fruit in a glass with a little of its liqueur.

Rinse and dry the cherries gently, and cut off the stalks to about 1 cm/½ inch. Halve the apricots and discard the stones.

Put the rum in a large bowl and stir in the sugar. Leave until dissolved, giving it a stir occasionally. Put the cherries or apricots into a sterilised container and cover with the liquid. As different fruit and flowers come into season, you add a layer, and keep topping up with fruit, flowers, sugar, and spirit throughout the summer and autumn.

Cook's tip

As you add more fruit, it is important to keep it covered in a mixture of spirit and sugar, in the proportions already given, 1 part floral sugar to 2 parts spirits and 2 parts fruit. If you prefer, grappa or *eau de vie de fruits* can replace the rum.

Peaches in clove carnation syrup

If you want to preserve ripe summer peaches for delicious desserts until the following summer, they should be processed in a boiling water bath – see p.33 – otherwise they will only keep for a couple of months. Peaches preserved in this way, as well as other fruit, such as apricots, cherries, and plums, can then be used in that lovely French batter pudding, *clafoutis*.

Make the scented syrup by putting the water and petals in a pan and bringing to the boil. Remove from the heat and leave the petals steeping until cold. Strain into a clean saucepan and add the sugar. Bring to the boil and remove from the heat.

Skin the peaches by putting them in a bowl and pouring boiling water over them. When cool enough to handle, slip the skins off, halve the fruit, and discard the stones.

Sterilise your glass preserving jars and lids – see p.30. Although the jars can be used again and again, the lid should be renewed each time you make a batch of fruit in syrup or similar preserves which are processed in a boiling water bath. It is important that there are no chips or cracks on the neck of the jar, as this would prevent a seal from forming.

Have ready a pan or stockpot with a lid, deep enough to take the lidded jars, standing on a trivet or rack to keep them away from the base of the pan. Failing all else, you can put a folded tea towel in the bottom of the pan.

Pack the fruit into two freshly sterilised preserving jars with the insides of the jars still

**makes 2 kg/4 lbs/
2 US quarts**

500 ml/17 fl oz/2 cups water
250 g/8 oz/1 cup scented
    clove pink or carnation
    petals
250 g/8 oz/1 cup sugar
1.5 kg/3 lbs firm but ripe
    peaches

wet, which helps to move the fruit around in the jar to pack it as firmly as possible without squashing it.

Pour the hot syrup over the fruit, ensuring there are no air bubbles. You can do this by gently shaking the jar to shift the fruit or by inserting a sterilised skewer or knife blade down the side of the jar wherever there are air bubbles. Add more syrup if necessary, so that it covers the fruit and reaches to the neck of the jar, but not far enough for it to touch the lid.

Wipe the rim of the jar, place the lids on, and seal the jars. If using the screw band, give it a quarter turn to loosen it so that steam can escape during the sterilization process.

Put the jars in the saucepan, ensuring that they do not touch each other – you can wrap the jars separately in folded newspaper. Fill the pan with water to the level of the syrup in the jar. Have a kettle of water ready to boil for topping up as the water evaporates. Put the saucepan on the heat, cover with the lid, and gently bring to the boil. Once the water boils, keep it boiling for 30 minutes (500 g/1 lb jars of produce only need 25 minutes from boiling), topping up with boiling water from the kettle, if necessary.

Once the jars have been processed, take the pan off the heat, remove the jars from the pan with tongs, and transfer them to a rack or wooden board. Immediately tighten the lids if using screw tops and leave the jars to cool completely. As the contents go cold, they shrink slightly and a vacuum is formed, creating sterile anaerobic or oxygen-free conditions in which bacteria do not survive.

Two Pigs Farm maple saffron pears and walnuts

Every year I receive a quart bottle of Two Pigs Farm maple syrup from my friend who owns the farm in Vermont and makes the syrup. Occasionally, when the new 'vintage' arrives, I have still have some left from the previous year, which I feel I can use more liberally, and I find it makes the most beautiful preserves.

Peel the pears. If they are small and neat enough to fit in the jar as such, leave them whole with the stalk attached. Otherwise, halve them and discard the core. As you prepare them, put them in a bowl with the lemon juice, coating them well to prevent them browning. Once all the pears are prepared, put half of them in a heatproof strainer with half the walnuts and place in a saucepan of boiling water for 20 seconds. Drain and pack into one of the jars. Blanch the second batch in the same way and pack into the second jar, distributing the allspice berries amongst the pears as you pack them into the jars.

Pound the saffron in a pestle. Pour on 2 tablespoons of boiling water and let this steep for about 20 minutes. Bring the maple syrup to the boil and stir in the saffron liquid. Pour the syrup over the pears and walnuts. Seal completely and process as in the previous recipe.

The pears will keep for a year, and can be used to fill tarts, but are also excellent served with roast duck or roast venison.

Cook's tip

If maple syrup is not available, make up a thick syrup with light brown sugar.

makes 2 kg/4 lbs/ 1 US quart

2 kg/4 lbs firm but ripe pears of even size, small rather than large, such as Bosc or Bartlett
Juice of 1 lemon
24 fresh walnut halves
12 allspice berries
1 generous pinch of saffron – 20 or more threads
500 ml/17 fl oz/2 cups maple syrup

Orange flower scented kumquats

This is a fabulous preserve to have in your pantry as it makes an instant dessert for a special occasion, with or without the best vanilla ice cream you can find.

Wash, scrub, and dry the fruit, prick all over and pack into sterilised preserving jars. Make a strong syrup with the sugar and water, remove from the heat, and stir in the orange flower water and the orange liqueur. Half-fill the jars with this syrup. Top up with vodka, seal, and label. After two or three months you will have delicious fruit to add to fruit salads, and a wonderful liqueur to use in cocktails.

makes 1 kg/2 lbs/1 US quart

1 kg/2 lbs kumquats
500 g/1 lb/2 cups granulated sugar
250 ml/8 fl oz/1 cup water
2 tablespoons orange flower water
125 ml/4 fl oz/½ cup orange liqueur such as Grand Marnier, Curaçao, or Cointreau
Vodka – see recipe

Tapenade

This rich, piquant paste, traditionally made with capers, called *tapéno* in Provençal, black olives and olive oil, to which I also add a hint of lavender, is delicious served with freshly baked or toasted country bread. Try mixing it with breadcrumbs and spreading over a rack of lamb before roasting it, or on a fillet of fish before grilling it.

Blend the capers, olives, and lavender with half the olive oil to a not-too-fine mixture in the food processor. Spoon into small sterilised jars, ensuring there are no air pockets, and fill to within about 1 cm/½ inches. of the top of the jars. Spoon a little olive oil on top, which will seal the mixture, and put on the jar lids. The tapenade will keep in the fridge for several weeks. For longer storage, add all the olive oil when blending the capers, olives, and lavender,

makes 500 g/1 lb/2 cups

250 g/8 oz/1 cup capers, well rinsed
250 g/8 oz/1 cup chopped pitted black olives
6 tablespoons extra-virgin olive oil
¼ teaspoon lavender flowers

then process the jars in a water bath, following the method on p.33. 125 g/4 oz jars will need only 15 minutes processing.

Wild garlic flower pesto

For me, this pesto has a particularly English flavour, so I use butter instead of olive oil. One of the finest Italian chefs I know, Mauro Bregoli from Emilia-Romagna, used to make pesto for his restaurant on the edge of the New Forest and he used butter, without the gods of *la cucina italiana* striking him down. Butter is the perfect vehicle for preserving the scent and flavour of the delicate wild garlic flowers, which olive oil might overwhelm.

Apart from the traditional use with pasta, try this stirred into mashed potatoes or on warm vegetable dishes. And for a sublime breakfast, spoon a little inside egg coddlers before cooking the eggs. Wild garlic coddled eggs with sourdough soldiers also makes a delightful first course or light lunch dish.

Make sure the wild garlic flowers are dry. Roughly chop them in a food processor. Add the walnuts, butter, and cheese, and blend until the mixture reaches the texture you prefer. Alternatively, pound the nuts with a pestle and mortar and then blend in the butter and very finely chopped wild garlic flowers. You can add a touch of grated nutmeg and/or freshly ground black pepper, if you like.

Store in small jars and keep refrigerated. If I make larger quantities, I freeze the pesto in ice cube trays and then store the frozen chunks in a bag in the freezer.

makes three 125 g/4 oz jars

75 g/3 oz wild garlic flowers and stalks

150 g/6 oz /1 cup walnut pieces

125 g/4 oz/1 stick butter, softened

125 g/4 oz/1 cup grated or crumbled mild Lancashire cheese

Sage flower and hazelnut pesto

Make sure the flowers and leaves are dry. Roughly chop them in a food processor. Add the rest of the ingredients, and blend until the mixture reaches the texture you prefer. Store in small jars and keep refrigerated. As in the previous recipe, if made in larger quantities, the pesto can be frozen in ice cube trays and the frozen chunks stored in a bag in the freezer.

makes three 125 g/4 oz jars

3 or 4 heaped tablespoons sage flowers
3 sage leaves
150 g/6 oz/1 cup blanched and skinned hazelnuts
175 ml/6 fl oz/¾ cup cold-pressed rapeseed oil or extra-virgin olive oil
125 g/4 fl oz/1 cup grated hard sheep cheese

Fennel flower and almond pesto

Make sure the flower heads are dry. Roughly chop them in a food processor. Add the rest of the ingredients and blend until the mixture reaches the texture you prefer. Store in small jars and keep refrigerated. As above, if made in larger quantities, the pesto can be frozen in ice cube trays and the frozen chunks stored in a bag in the freezer.

Cook's tip

Try this pesto stirred into sautéed prawns and courgettes and tossed with freshly cooked pasta.

makes three 125 g/4 oz jars

20 fennel flower heads, including fresh seed pods, if there are any 150 g/ 6 oz/1 cup blanched and skinned almonds
175 ml/6 fl oz/¾ cup extra-virgin olive oil
125 g/4 fl oz/1 cup grated Parmesan

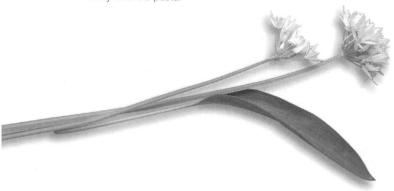

Golden pesto

Make sure the flower heads are dry. Roughly chop them in a food processor. Add the almonds, butter, and Cheddar, and process for 30 seconds or so before adding the saffron and its liquid, then blend the mixture until it reaches the texture you prefer. Store in small jars and keep refrigerated. As with the other similar recipes, if made in larger quantities, the pesto can be frozen in ice cube trays and the frozen chunks stored in a bag in the freezer.

Cook's tip

Try this summery pesto with risotto. It is also wonderful stirred into mashed potatoes or served with fish cakes.

makes three 125 g/4 oz jars

4 or 5 heaped tablespoons mixed golden edible flower petals — fennel flowers, day lilies, nasturtiums, and marigolds
150 g/6 oz /1 cup blanched and skinned almonds
125 g/4 oz/1 stick softened butter
125 g/4 oz/1 cup grated Cheddar
Pinch of saffron threads soaked in 1 tablespoon boiling water

Elderflower-cured mackerel

This is based on the classic recipe for curing raw fish, in which I replace the dill with elderflowers.

Remove as many bones from the fillets as possible. Mix the salt, sugar, pepper, and vodka or gin to make the marinade.

Put two elderflower heads in the bottom of a rectangular dish large enough to take four pieces of fish. Spoon a quarter of the marinade over the flowers and lay four pieces of fish on top of them, skin-side down.

Spread half of the remaining mixture on the flesh side of each mackerel fillet and sandwich with the remaining four fillets, placing two more elderflower heads between.

The remaining marinade is spread on the skin side of the top fillets, with the remaining

serves 8

8 mackerel fillets
5 tablespoons sea salt
2 tablespoons light brown sugar
1 tablespoon freshly ground black pepper
2 tablespoons vodka or cucumber, elderflower and lemon gin (p.113)
6 elderflower heads

elderflowers on top. Cover with cling film, weight down, and refrigerate for at least 24 hours and up to 3 days.

To serve, scrape off the curing ingredients, drain off the liquid, and slice the fish. Mackerel is not as firm as salmon, so I find it preferable to slice in relatively thick vertical slices down to the skin.

Cook's tip

As an accompaniment, I suggest a home-made mayonnaise flavoured with elderflower. An apple, fennel, and walnut salad is the perfect accompaniment, or try the mackerel with a gooseberry chutney.

Wild garlic flower and ginger cured mackerel

The subtle Oriental flavours can be used with any of the oily fish, from sardines to salmon; I first developed the recipe in Hong Kong, using flowering garlic chives (*gau tsoi fa*).

Remove as many bones from the fillets as possible. Mix the rest of the ingredients, except the flowering stalks, to make the marinade.

Put four flowers in the bottom of a rectangular dish large enough to take four mackerel fillets. Spoon a quarter of the marinade over the flowers and lay four fillets on top of them, skin-side down.

Spread half of the remaining mixture on the flesh side of each mackerel fillet and sandwich with the remaining four fillets, with four more flower heads between.

The remaining marinade is spread on the skin side of the top fillets, with the remaining wild

serves 8

8 mackerel fillets

3 tablespoons sea salt

2 tablespoons light brown sugar

1 tablespoon soy sauce

1 tablespoon freshly ground black pepper

2 teaspoons freshly grated ginger

2 tablespoons fino sherry

12 wild garlic flower heads and stalks

garlic flowers on top. Cover with cling film, weight down, and refrigerate for at least 24 hours and up to 3 days.

To serve, scrape off the curing ingredients, drain off the liquid, and slice the fish in thick vertical slices down to the skin.

Cook's tip

As an accompaniment, I suggest a dipping sauce flavoured with wild garlic flower vinegar (p.139) or lime juice, a little more grated ginger, 1 teaspoon of honey and a splash of soy sauce.

Jasmine tea cured salmon

I learned to use tea as an ingredient many years ago with Bruce Cost in San Francisco, tea-smoked salmon and tea-cured salmon being particular favourites. It was a short step to move on to jasmine tea, with added jasmine flowers for this delicate and subtly flavoured salmon, versions of which appeared in more than one of my newspaper columns over the years.

Have the fish scaled before dividing into two neat fillets. Remove as many bones from the fillets as possible. Mix the salt, sugar, peppers, and rice wine. Fino or dry Amontillado sherry could replace the rice wine, if you prefer.

Spread 1 tablespoon of tea leaves and a third of the jasmine flowers in the bottom of a rectangular dish, large enough to take the piece of fish. Spoon 3 tablespoons of marinade over the leaves, and lay one piece of fish on top, skin-side down.

Spread the half of the remaining mixture on the flesh side of each fillet of salmon and sandwich

serves 8

1 salmon tail piece, weighing about 1 kg/2 lbs

5 tablespoons coarse sea salt

2 tablespoons light brown sugar

1 tablespoon freshly ground black pepper

1 tablespoon Sichuan peppercorns, crushed

2 to 3 tablespoons mirin, sake, or rice wine

4 to 5 tablespoons jasmine tea plus 1 tablespoon of dried jasmine flowers

the two together with half the remaining tea leaves and jasmine flowers between.

The rest of the salt and pepper mixture should be spread on the skin side of the top fillet, and the rest of the tea-leaves and flowers sprinkled on top. Cover with cling film, weight down, and refrigerate for 2 to 3 days and up to 6.

To serve, scrape off the curing ingredients, drain off the liquid, and slice the salmon, either in small, thick, vertical slices down to the skin, or on the diagonal.

Cook's tip

As an accompaniment, I suggest a home-made mayonnaise flavoured with lime juice and zest, a little wasabi paste or horseradish, some grated ginger, and a little jasmine syrup (p.101).

Lavender-cured trout

Brown trout and rainbow trout can sometimes be a little lacking in flavour. Try this for a striking way of preserving with a floral flavour.

Mix the salt, sugar, pepper, lavender, and vermouth.

Spread 1 tablespoon of the marinade in the bottom of a rectangular dish, large enough to take 4 fillets. Use all but 2 tablespoons of the marinade to sandwich each pair of fillets and place in the dish. The remaining marinade should be lightly spread on the skin side of the top fillets. Cover with film, weight down, and refrigerate for 2 to 3 days and up to 6.

To serve, scrape off the curing ingredients, drain off the liquid, and cut each fillet diagonally in three for serving.

serves 8

4 small to medium rainbow or brown trout, filleted and pin bones removed

6 tablespoons coarse sea salt

3 tablespoons light brown sugar

1 tablespoon freshly ground black pepper

1 ½ teaspoons lavender flowers

3 tablespoons dry white vermouth

Flower ices and sorbets

Note that ice cream recipes use raw eggs. And also remember to remove the ices from the freezer for 10 to 15 minutes before serving.

Rose and raspberry ice cream

Apricots with lavender sugar, cherries with clove, carnation sugar, or syrup (see pp.25–26), and gooseberries with elderflower syrup (see p.101) can be made into floral fruit ice creams using this same recipe.

Gently cook the raspberries with the citrus zest and half the sugar until they collapse, 3 to 4 minutes only, in fact hardly enough to cook them, just to heat them through. Remove the lemon and orange zests and sieve the purée. Heat the milk and cream in a saucepan. In a bowl, beat together the eggs, remaining sugar. and glucose, if using it. When warm, add a quarter of the cream mixture to the beaten eggs and thoroughly incorporate. When the remaining cream boils, pour it over the egg mixture, beating continuously.

Sieve the egg and cream mixture into a clean saucepan and cook gently until it will coat the back of a spoon. Cool, stir in the rose and raspberry purée, then freeze in a *sorbetière*, ice cream maker, or freezer container.

Cook's tip

Serve the ice cream in cornets, and arrange bouquet fashion in a container, or serve scoops on shortbread biscuits, with extra fruit purée.

serves 6

375 g/12 oz/1 ½ cups raspberries, rinsed

Thinly pared zest of ½ lemon and ½ orange

250 g/8 oz/1 cup rose petal sugar (p.25)

250 ml/8 fl oz/1 cup milk

250 ml/8 fl oz /1 cup single or double cream

6 egg yolks

1 tablespoon glucose (optional, for extra smoothness)

Mango, lime, and jasmine kulfi

Apart from tomatoes, sardines, chickpeas, and tuna, my kitchen cupboard contains few cans. It was years before I discovered the properties of condensed and evaporated milk, and now I would not be without them. Slow-cooked milk is a feature of desserts not only in Latin America, with *dulce de leche* and *cajeta,* but also the Indian sub-continent. Here the work is all done for you in this luscious floral tropical ice.

Empty the contents of the cans into a bowl and whisk well to combine the very different textures. Peel and purée the mangoes, keeping back 8 thin slices for decoration, then mix thoroughly into the milk mixture together with the lime zest and juice and the jasmine syrup. Pour it either into 8 moulds or into a shallow, rectangular container, so that you will get something about 4 cm/1 ½ inches deep, and will be able to cut into 8 portions. Freeze for several hours, until thick but not hard. Break up the mixture and put it in the food processor for a minute or so, processing until smooth, then refreeze until ready to use. Turn out, or cut up, and decorate each portion with a thin curl of peeled mango, and, if you have the time, crystallised jasmine flowers.

serves 8

1 large can sweetened condensed milk (approx. 400 ml/14 fl oz)
1 large can evaporated milk (approx. 400 ml/14 fl oz)
2 large ripe mangoes
Finely grated zest of 2 limes
Juice of 2 limes
2 tablespoons jasmine syrup – see p. 101

Jasmine and ginger ice cream

Fragrance and heat characterize this ice cream, which is a perfect ending to a meal with Asian or Oriental flavours. There is, indeed, a generous helping of ginger, but freezing tames it.

Simmer the ginger in the syrup for 5 minutes. Remove the pan from the heat. Scald the milk in a separate saucepan, remove from the heat, and stir in the ginger and jasmine syrup. Infuse for about an hour and do not strain at this stage.

Proceed with the ice cream making in the usual way, re-heating the milk and syrup mixture before pouring it on the beaten egg yolks to make the custard. Stir this over a very low heat until it thickens just enough to coat the back of a spoon, but without letting it curdle. The ginger is removed when the custard is strained before the addition of the cream, and the mixture is then frozen. For a more intense flavour, press the ginger in the sieve.

Cook's tip

Once the ice cream is made, you can freeze it in a lined Swiss roll tray and then cut out rounds to sandwich between thin almond biscuits or brandy snap wafers for an unusual dessert.

serves 8

75 g/3 oz/¼ cup fresh ginger, peeled and finely chopped
250 ml/8 fl oz/1 cup jasmine syrup (p.101)
375 ml/13 fl oz/1 ½ cups full cream milk
6 egg yolks, beaten together
250 ml/8 fl oz/1 cup whipping cream

Lavender and blueberry sorbet

This deep purple ice cream is very dramatic to look at as well as to taste. A small scoop of it transforms a homely blueberry crumble into a very special dessert.

Make a syrup of the grape juice and sugar and bring to the boil. Put the lemon zest with the lavender flowers in the boiling syrup. Leave to infuse for an hour or so. Stir in the lemon juice, strain the infusion, and put in a blender with the blueberries. Blend until smooth. Strain and freeze the mixture in a *sorbetière*, ice cream maker, or freezer container.

serves 6 to 8

500 ml/17 fl oz/2 cups red grape juice
250 g/8 oz/1 cup granulated sugar
Zest of 1 lemon in thin strips
Juice of 1 lemon
1 to 2 teaspoons lavender flowers, tied in muslin
500 g/1 lb/2 cups blueberries

Linden flower and lime sorbet

This simple sorbet can be served very soft, in a wine glass, with a splash of grappa or vodka for an instant dessert, or without the spirit as a refreshing cooler on a hot day.

Thinly pare off the lime zest and put it with the linden flowers in a pitcher. Boil the water and pour it over the flowers and zest. Leave to infuse for 10 minutes. Stir in the lime juice and sugar, and, when this has dissolved, strain the infusion, cool, and freeze in a *sorbetière*, ice cream maker, or freezer container. If the latter, to ensure a smooth texture, you will need to stir the freezing mixture from time to time. Alternatively, scrape the frozen mixture with a fork, scoop into a glass, and enjoy the fragrance of summer as it melts on your tongue.

serves 4 to 6

1 lime
3 tablespoons linden flowers
375 ml/13 fl oz/1 ½ cups water
250 g/8 oz/1 cup sugar

Index